1970

To Jim

Renegades is a renegade sport. It's been a sort of "crazy people change the world." Hope this little book triggers some nostalgia and your own fun stories.

Good memories
Good friends
Good fun

Rosie Harreveld Clark

Keep da curl

Let's Go, Let's Go!

Let's Go, Let's Go! is published by
Harrison Clark, 850 5th Lane N.W.
Choteau, MT 59422
(406) 466-2072

Cover art by Country Rose
Photos by Doc Ball, LeRoy Grannis,
Clarence Maki, John Russell, Craig Stecyk,
George Steinmetz, Ron Stoner, Jean Paul Van Swae,
Pierre "The Fly" Van Swae and others,
courtesy of the Harrison Family Collection

Book design by Jeffrey Girard and George Pryor,
Victoria Street Graphic Design, San Clemente, California

Hardcover: ISBN# 0-9660153-1-2
Softcover ISBN# 0-9660153-2-0
Printed in the USA

LET'S GO, LET'S GO!

The biography of
Lorrin "Whitey" Harrison:
California's Legendary
Surf Pioneer

by Rosie Harrison Clark

This book is dedicated to Cecelia Harrison
and the entire Harrison family.

*Thank you to all of the very special friends and family
that so generously lent me their support and "Lorrin"
stories. Big thank yous to Barbara Melton who spent
many hours in front of her computer deciphering my
semi-legible handwriting, to Paul Zarzyski for his off-
the-board literary genius, to Jeff Girard who tied up
all the loose ends into one beautiful bundle, to Steve
Pezman for holding my hand, and of course my three
sisters, Ginger, Marian and Jennie.*

Mahalo,

CONTENTS

IV Prologue

2 The Extrovert

30 Above All, Have Fun

43 Tarzan Slept In My Bed

66 Paradise

95 Surfer's Daughter

122 Who Can Say They Surfed
In A Hurricane

142 Stoked

Baby's first wave. Ginger and Daddy Lorrin at Dana Point, 1937.

P R O L O G U E

THE WHITE SAND FELT WARM against my bare skin as I nestled sleepily into it. "Rosie, Let's go. Let's go!"

I looked up into the sun-drenched face. Below a shock of light golden curl, pale blue eyes laughed and crinkled down at me. A row of absolutely straight white teeth shone from lips too sunburned to ever quite complete a full smile. His lean, muscular body was of burnt umber with salt-dried droplets clinging to it.

At four years of age I squirmed deeper into the sand knowing I could not avoid the inevitable. Looking out at the sun glistening on the beckoning surf, with total enthusiasm he swept me up in one arm and hefted his surfboard over his shoulder with the other.

Lying in a tandem prone position we glided swiftly over the glassy swells, propelled by arms made strong by the sea. Tiny sprays of bubbles swept over the deck of the heavy redwood board. It quickly beaded up on the highly varnished surface, feeling cool to my small body. The wave rising toward us opened wide like a large dark chasm threatening to swallow us. A little whimper of fear escaped me as I gripped the redwood rails and raised my chest up to meet it. "Hang on," he said as he held me tight. It toppled over just a little at the top, white froth flowing over us as we smacked down on the back side of the wave.

The other surfers shouted "Outside," and we all paddled like crazy to get out beyond the break. Suddenly he sat up, turned the board around quickly, heading toward shore. He said, "Paddle, Rosie, it's a good one. With teeth chattering and arms barely able to reach over the rails, I paddled as hard as I could. "Harder now!" and I could feel the back of the board raise up on the wave. In one deft movement he was standing, holding me securely in front of him, sliding at a right angle against a smooth green swell. A curl of white water followed us. My feet barely touched the board as he held me close. Then, up I went to his shoulders. There was no other feeling like this. I was on top of the world. All of my fears were dispelled in a moment as we sped toward shore, wind and spray in our faces. I only felt complete trust and love for this man that held me aloft so effortlessly.

When the wave died out he sat me back down on the board. I said, "Let's go again, Daddy." For I am a surfer's daughter and this is my first recollection of life and it was the same for my brothers and sisters.

I'm not sure when my first wave was, maybe three months or three weeks old, but it was an ever exciting, slightly frightening, wonderful experience.

The Extrovert

C H A P T E R   I

His name was Lorrin "Whitey" Harrison, legendary pioneer of the sport of surfing, commercial fisherman, diver, outrigger canoeman. He spent his life in and around the sea and shared his love for it and its lessons with all that knew him.

In the early '90s he gained a sort of celebrity status. At 80 years of age his perpetual enthusiasm, whether it be weaving a palm frond hat, strumming a tune on his ukulele, or just getting stoked on a two-foot wave, seemed to be contagious to all ages. He did several commercials for companies such as Nike, Budget Rent-a-Car, and Armor All. He was dubbed "The Armor All Man."

In 1984 he suffered a major heart attack and underwent quadruple bypass surgery. I was with him that day for the outrigger canoe races at Mission Bay in San Diego. He kept telling me that it felt like someone was sitting on his chest. After each race he was determined to help carry every canoe up the beach.

It was hard to hold him down. When he was lying in that hospital bed with everything stuck into him, he assured us that we should not be unhappy for him. "I've had a good life, the best," but he wasn't done yet! The nurse found him standing on the hospital bed, tubes hanging from him all over the place, using the urinal. He said he couldn't do it lying down.

During the surgery they had some complications. Afterward the doctor carefully explained to us that there was a possibility of brain damage. My stepmother, Cecelia, and I spent a fitful night and went to see him in the morning just feeling sick that he might not be normal. He wasn't! As soon as we opened the door to the large room occupied by many patients in various stages of recovery, we could hear his voice loud and clear. He was telling everyone who would listen, "It was just like when I was diving over one hundred feet and lost my air. Had to hold my breath for a long time until I reached the surface."

Two months later a friend called me and said "Hey, I just saw your dad surfing on TV." From that day on I think he tried to live every day to the max. He was featured in *Life* magazine, on the David Letterman Show, Tom Brokaw, David Brinkley, *Invention*, and more that I can't remember.

While filming the thirty-second Armor All segment, they asked if he could stay out surfing for one hour. He stayed out there six hours, in good-sized waves, catching one after another. He told me, "I got tired." I said, "Geez, Daddy, take it easy, after all, you are eighty years old now." He never did. He just laughed and hammed it up for the cameras. They even had a registered nurse on the beach for him.

A true extrovert, he loved nothing more than showing off his talents and abilities. He certainly wasn't anything like all of my friends' fathers. Usually he was barefoot or wearing thong sandals, a pair of well worn paint-stained jeans, an aloha shirt or no shirt at all, and a coconut hat. He was a hero to me as most fathers are to little kids, but then he was just Daddy.

Like most teenagers, when I reached that precarious age I had to take him down off of that hero pedestal for a while. It was the 1950s and most kids were arguing about what they wanted to wear or if they could drive the car. I was complaining about the surfboards he made. They were

Original pier at Dana, 1937. Lorrin and Ginger on the surfboard "Waikiki."

First place paddleboard contest Santa Monica. Lorrin and Baby Rosie, 1940.

too big, not the right shape, too long, not in style. It didn't
deter him at all. He went right on inventing and developing
all kinds of boards, all of which I thought not perfect at
the time. Now I can laugh at my frustrated teen years and
realize what an innovator he truly was. He actually built
the first foam surfboard. Like many inventors, he was more
compulsive about his creations than he was concerned
about the long-term credit he might have achieved.

We owned a 1936 Ford sedan convertible. Ford grey
was the "in" color. Since I was born in 1940 and this
was a beach buggy, it was well broken in by 1943, as I recall.
My dad was working lifeguard at Santa Monica. There was
always fishing gear of some kind laying around. Feather
jigs were my favorite: little brass bodies with ruby red eyes
and white chicken feathers. We spent evenings polishing
them. Actually they were made as lures to represent squid.

One used to be able to drive out on the piers in
California. We were leaving the Santa Monica pier and the
other lifeguards watched, laughing, as my sister, Ginger,
and I decided to drop the weights out of the convertible.
They were on long fishing lines coiled up behind the back
seat by the window—if you could call those little oval
isinglass things windows. Ours was missing, so the weights
and lines fit right through. It was fun to watch them bounce
down the highway as we turned the corners and released
more line. We went quite a ways before Daddy caught on.

The back seat of the old bathtub-shaped vehicle was
reserved for kids and surfboards. Ginger and I rode on top
of four to six big planks that weren't always tied down. We
would slide down them or topple off onto the seat or floor
boards as they slid from side to side when we went around
corners. Often we crawled underneath them to play or sleep.

Ginger, the hula girl, four years old.

Rigging the canoe, San Onofre, 1940. Lorrin and Rosie, Yann Egasse and Ginger.
'36 Ford convertible in background.

Of course the old car always quit on us when we were
ascending a hill. Daddy called people right off the side-
walks in Laguna to help. All passengers bailed out to push
it over the top. When it got to rolling good he jumped in
and started it with us all trailing behind. If it was cool we
had an old army blanket or quilt to put over us. There were
always some in the back seat to put between the boards
with a few left over. One day we were driving down the
Coast Highway in the middle of Laguna when the blanket
blew off us kids and flew over Daddy's head, blinding him.
He hollered, "What the heck? I can't see a thing," before
he managed to struggle free without having a wreck.

I was four and one half and Ginger was eight when our
mother died of a sudden illness. We were living in Costa
Mesa at the time. I have snips of memories of her. She had
red hair, helped me dress my dolls, led me to town in the

Lorrin Sr. with Jennie on shoulders, Marian and Lorrin Jr.
Cecelia on the right at Canoes, Waikiki, 1955.

wagon pulled by a shaggy little dog. She even took the big fish hook out of my hand that I had fallen on in the back yard. Because I was so young, I am sure losing her was much harder on Ginger than it was on me.

In the evenings the rattan furniture with hibiscus upholstery seemed to always be filled with people laughing and singing. Invariably someone would want Ginger and me to do the hula while our Dad played the guitar and sang.

Mel Butts was a fisherman and a cartoonist of sorts. I liked the little sleepy Mexicans he drew. One day we were moored in the bay while all the guys were cleaning a particularly large catch of fish. Ginger and I were sitting on the cabin of the fishing boat. This was our usual spot to sit so that we would be out of the way. This particular day it was extra fun because they had caught a baby seal and tied it to the boat. As we two little girls watched the seal

Little Lorrin, Marian and Jennie stroking.   *1947, first hats, here with baby Marian.*

Ginger, Dana, 1938, sporting seaweed skirt.

play and dive in the water, no one noticed that I slipped off of the cabin and fell in. No one except Mel Butts, that is. Now Mel had his hip boots on and rolled down, but he went right in after me. With my eyes wide open I saw the thick braided rope bumper hanging on the side of the boat. I made a grab for it and clung on tight. I watched as Mel went sailing right down beside me straight to the bottom. When everyone had realized what had happened, it was easy to pull me out by the rope, but Mel was a different story, with those big boots filled with water. Half of the crew jumped overboard to help him. The other half waited until they hauled him up over the boat rail. Sputtering and laughing, he made sure that I was okay, then he sat down, pulled those boots off and poured out what seemed like a gallon of water from each one. Well, that entire event called for a big fish fry and party at our house, more story telling, and Mel drew cartoons for me and Ginger.

Today my kids and grandkids wonder how I know so many old Hawaiian songs. My life was filled with music. My dad loved to sing and play his guitar and ukulele. He first went to Hawaii when he was eighteen years old. He stowed away aboard a cruise liner, but was caught just off Diamond Head and was shipped back home before his feet ever touched Hawaiian soil. That was in the early '30s when it was not uncommon for people to ride the rails and stow away. Penalties weren't so great because times were tough and people couldn't afford to travel. When he got home he went right back and did it again. This time he was caught, but they put him to work. What could be better. He was in Hawaii and had a job too. He bunked at the Waikiki bachelor quarters and made friends with all the Hawaiian beachboys. They nicknamed him "Whitey" because of his blond hair. He surfed boards and outriggers with them and even dove for pennies when the cruise ships came in. In the evenings they would sit on the beach and jam for hours playing all the popular Hawaiian tunes of that era.

He grew up in the Santa Ana Canyon in California. His parents also owned a beach house at Sleepy Hollow, Laguna Beach, where the family spent summers when he was a child. He had two older brothers and a little sister, Ethel. He and Ethel were so close in age they were almost like twins, and both of them learned to love to surf, a sport that was to belong to a select few for many years. His mother was very religious and made sure the children went to church on Sundays and practiced piano every day. Well, Daddy was the rebellious one and was always running off to go surfing as soon as he was old enough to do so, and he usually conned Ethel into going with him.

Old Corona del Mar surfer, Ned Leutzinger, claims, "Lorrin was the craziest friend I ever had. Why, one time when he was just in high school Lorrin got up in the middle of the night and rode the old family horse from his house to his girl friend, Helen Harper's house. She was asleep on the back porch, so he just tied up the horse and climbed into bed with her."

He tells the story of high school graduation day: "That morning Lorrin and I got a ride early to Laguna to go fishing in his brother Winfred's boat. The barracuda were running and we thought we had plenty of time. We did catch one really big one and decided to call it quits. We had to hitch-hike home to Orange. Several hours went by before we caught a ride. Lorrin just missed his graduation, but accepted his diploma backstage. With his big barracuda wrapped in newspaper in one hand, he shook hands with the principal and received his diploma with the other. Needless to say his mother, father, aunts and uncles that had come to watch were less than pleased."

"Kookbox" paddleboard races, 1940s.

Early fishing days.

The note read "The Big Ones are Humping." The teacher wanted to know why Lorrin was absent the day before and the meaning of the note, but he wouldn't say a thing, so was sent to the principal. Upon questioning he replied, "It means just what it says," and was expelled from school for two weeks. He always told us it was the best two weeks of surfing he ever had. That was before they put the breakwater in at Corona Del Mar and that was

"the surfing spot." They even had to walk to it because the coast highway didn't go by it then. Not too many years later the waves were ruined by the building of the break-water. They were into big heavy long boards and long rides. They had to search elsewhere for a new surfing beach.

San Onofre became the Mecca for this small band of surfing junkies. Actually I never knew what most of them did for a living. The ocean is one of those real equalizers.

Stripped down to a pair of trunks and a surfboard with nothing else between one and the elements, affluence and monetary values account for little.

I loved all those old guys with their colorful nicknames. They were so good to us two little girls. They carefully baby-sat and tended to us while we played on the beach. Knowing that we were missing a mother they all took a hand at being one. They were like family.

"Pop" Proctor was retired and lived in his old van at 'Nofre. He started surfing when he was sixty years old. He was the oldest. Not having children of his own, he raised several boys. "The Viking" I remember most. There were rarely any other kids at the beach so even though he was older than us we found him interesting. He was lean with dark hair and tanned skin. Pop taught him to surf and fish and respect the sea. We liked to follow him around and watch him catch baby octopus in the tide pools. Guess Pop did a good job. The Viking grew up to be a very professional person.

"Kioki" had only one good eye due to a car accident. Being a magician, he would eat starfish, sea shells, kelp balls, or whatever we would bring him. He made them disappear and reappear for us like magic.

Eddie McBride was one of my favorites. A short brown bear of a man, black hair curling all over his body and a big white smile laughing from under a broad-brimmed tightly woven straw hat. He usually had a bottle wrapped in a brown paper sack in one hand that he took a swig from now and then.

"Opai" was the kid. "Opai means shrimp. He probably was in his late teens or early twenties. There was Card, Peanuts with his woody station wagon, Hammerhead, Burrhead, Huckleberry, Fritz, Windy, to name a few. They were regulars and often would spend the entire weekend at

Publicity photo shoot for the starlets. Santa Monica Lifeguards.

Corona del Mar gang—winter warmup.

Confirmed wave watchers. Rosie, Rosie, Fritz.

Surfing orphans. Rosie and Ginger, 1945.

San Onofre, riding the waves, telling stories around the fire pit, drinking, dancing, singing, and crashing on the beach or retiring to their panel trucks and wagons.

I suppose those bottles in the brown bags were intriguing to a five-year-old. One evening my dad found me down the beach a ways, passed out in the sand after indulging in sneaking sips out of most everyone's bottles. The next day he carefully explained why I should never do such a thing again. I was pretty good about it but I loved the taste of beer and would con someone into giving me an occasional sip. Though in all probability they were a band of drunken renegades, I certainly didn't see them in that light.

Lots of socializing takes place while waiting for the right wave. Sometimes it's quite a while between sets. On a glassy sunshiny day, this is an almost mesmerizing form of physical therapy. Sitting there in the warm summer currents swinging your legs to stay in position, occasionally pulling a hand through the water, drifting like sitting ducks on a pond, one could almost fall asleep.

It was just such a fine day as we sat there waiting for our wave listening to outrageous story telling. My dad quietly warned me that we would stay as far away as possible from Brignell. He wore coke bottle glasses and rode a big hollow paddle board. I believe they called him "Nelly Bly." That day it seemed that he was always beside us. He must have been close to legally blind, because when we took off on that just right wave, he cut right into us. Before fiberglass and gel coats we didn't use so much wax on the boards and the varnish was fairly slick. Well, my dad never used much wax anyway. I think his feet were so abrasive they just naturally stuck to any surface. When we wrecked with "Nelly Bly" I just slipped right off the board back into the wave. My dad caught me by the heel and it seemed like an eternity that I was being towed along under the water. He finally fished

Big boards and paddleboards of the '30s.

me out and let me cough and sputter awhile before we paddled back out to share this grand experience with the rest of the gang.

My youngest sister, Jennie, recently told me that she slipped right through his legs on a big wave at Dana when she was five years old. She just floated out there over the swells while he rode all the way to the beach without her then came back to pick her up. No problem! Mom was a little upset as she watched from the beach.

The summer of 1945 was the most memorable of my lifetime. Ginger was eight and I was five. We literally lived on the beach with our dad. During the winter our maternal grandmother kept us for him, but weekends and summers we were all his. He was fishing out of the cove between Dana Point and Doheny. "The Cove" was reserved for a few

Whitey, Waikiki beachboy, early 1930s.

fishermen. People could walk to it, but it was a difficult feat over the rocks. To me it seemed like a long way to drive to it from the coast highway. Winding around on a dirt road, you had to have a key to unlock the gate. We camped in an old army tent on a little rise just below the cliffs. Depending on the tide there was little or no beach, another reason why it didn't appeal to the public.

We would go fishing with him every day, play on the cliffs and learn about life and the sea. There was a large sandy spot where he launched his skiff. "Shuffle your feet" he would warn us, "Don't want a sting ray to get you." If you shuffled through the soft sand in the shallow warm water you would bump them and frighten them away. If you stepped on them they could lash their tail around and put a stinger right into you. We always shuffled and never got stung. Scary to me!

We would get in the little dinghy and row out to the "Soupfin," his fishing boat. Then we would carefully take the big boat out to sea between the rocks of the natural harbor. When the water was clear you could see many sting rays there. I don't recall ever fishing too far out. The coast line was always in sight.

When he pulled the lobster traps we could hardly wait to see what was in them. There were lots of species of ocean life in there besides the "bugs," most of which were not marketable at that time, so we ate well. In fact most of our meals were seafood. When Grandma had steak at her house and Ginger was very young she would say, "Pass the fish." Today all the sea creatures that we ate out of necessity are considered popular delicacies in the marketplace.

It was total darkness in the big tent as I crawled out of my bag and stumbled to the flap to see what the shouting and commotion was about. "Rosie, Ginger, the grunion are running. Help me catch 'em," my dad was yelling. Peering out I saw slivers of bright silver lights jumping and dancing along the beach with each incoming wave. Ginger was standing outside rubbing her eyes in disbelief at the sight of our dad stark naked in the bright moonlight at the edge of the water scooping up the tiny bouncing fish in a large tub.

The tide was high and the waves crashed up the beach with tremendous force. The tub washed toward the cliff with the incoming wave and back down the little shelf of beach on the back wash. "Hurry," he shouted as we stood there trance like in our brand new lacy Cinderella night-gowns that Grandma had just bought for us. Suddenly Ginger ran to the waters edge and bent over to scoop water and fish into her nightgown. Then she ran to deposit them in the tub. There were literally thousands upon thousands of the grunion shining and writhing upon the night blue moonlit sands. Soon I was involved in the same activity,

Anchored at the cove, now part of Dana Harbor.

Bringing in the haul at the end of the day.

1935, going to Hawaii in style. Ethel and Lorrin.

the nightgowns working quite well as a net. Running here and there laughing and slipping on the little fish bodies in our bare feet, we finally filled up several tubs. We began to see lights coming around the rocks from Doheny. Daddy yelled at us, "Hold this tub while I run to put some trunks on." We were close to the water's edge. Ginger was terrified that the tub and I were going to be swept out to sea before he got back as the tide was coming in and the waves washed up around us. The next day friends helped clean the fish and we had a big grunion fry. I was too exhausted to enjoy them or the party.

Often I think of whaler's children and other children who are allowed to join their fathers in the hunt. What seems perhaps sacrilege and waste to us today was acceptable then. Fishing shark was the most exciting of fishing trips. Ginger and I were ordered to sit on the boat cabin as our dad and Eric hauled in the large nets containing sharks of all kinds. Eric Hoguestrum was a Swede, with an old world accent and a deeply weathered face. He wove beautiful white fishing nets twenty to forty feet long. Weaving and knotting he deftly moved the wood shuttle to make the great pieces of macramé.

"This one's a big hammerhead" and we scrunched our knees up a little tighter to our chests as they threw the huge shark on the deck of the boat where it thrashed about until they killed it with large knives.

There were lots of different kinds, blue sharks, horned sharks, leopards, soup fins, threshers, hammerheads, and more big and small all netted and killed for just their livers. Shark liver oil was a much sought after commodity. The shark itself was not considered edible. I assume the practice either fell out of favor or the market dropped. My dad only fished them for a short time. He gave me horns from a horn shark as a gift.

He was fishing at "The Cove" and surfing at Doheny when he met Cecelia. She was a waitress at the Dana Villa. The Dana Villa has become a landmark. It is still there on the coast highway at the south entrance to the Dana Point Harbor.

Cecelia is a descendent of the Yorba family that originally owned one of the largest Spanish land grants in old California. She lived with her grandmother in the adobe Pryor homestead one half mile inland from Doheny. When her grandmother died, the house, which was built before the San Juan Capistrano Mission, was willed to her along with some acreage. I remember first meeting her. I thought she was very beautiful and I was shy and had difficulty talking in her presence. Her aunt and uncle and two cousins were living with her at the time. The youngest cousin, Butch, couldn't pronounce Cecelia so called her "Lele." To Ginger and me she was always Lele. It seemed a special name for her just for us. Now she is Grandma Lele for many grandchildren.

The Yorba family had an inherent fear of the ocean. Cecelia didn't even swim when my dad talked her into going surfing with him. That first ride resulted in a wreck. She fell on the board and cut her lip with her front teeth. But it didn't stop her. She and my father were married in 1946 and went to Hawaii for their honeymoon. Where else?

Abalones were in abundance in the lush kelp beds along the California sea coast. Lorrin Harrison was the most respected diver out there. However, it wasn't just the diving for them, prying them off the rocks and hauling them in that made his name synonymous with a good abalone steak. It was the processing of them, a procedure in which the meat was pried out of the shell, "shucked" and the entrails, "guts," removed. The outer layer was cut off with sharpened ham knives, "trimmed" all around from

Shuckin' abs.

The Cannery race, Newport Harbor.

Big bugs.

bottom to top. Then the heel and top were cut off leaving a good size chunk of firm white meat. This was then sliced into one half inch rounds to be "pounded" with large wooden mallets into tender steaks so delicate they resembled lace doilies. These were then carefully layered in wax paper in five-pound boxes ready for delivery to prestigious restaurants along the coast. It was not uncommon to see "Harrison Abalones" on the menu.

When he met Cecelia he was diving and processing out of the little cove where we had camped. After they were married they built a nice shop between the house and the barn and she helped him set up business. The shop had a large high rectangular table that many hands could stand around and trim. There were meat slicers, concrete blocks to pound on and freezers to put the "abs" in. It was a busy time. A day could start at 5 a.m. to go out diving and if they had a good day it wasn't uncommon for the processing to last until 2 or 3 a.m. Many of the restaurants insisted on fresh abs instead of frozen. It was important that this process be completed as quickly as possible in order that the abalones retain that rich, delicate flavor.

Lele was prone to sea sickness so she stayed off the boat as much as possible but kept the business at home running smoothly. Many of the surfing gang got involved in it. Some stayed on longer than others. Voss and Margret Harrington worked for them on weekends, Voss diving and Margret processing. They ran the business while Lorrin and Cecelia went on their honeymoon to Hawaii. Dave and Paula Tompkins were partners with Daddy and Lele for a while. Rennie Yater dove for them sometimes. "Flippy" Hoffman started his own business.

When we had a particularly big haul, my dad would call more friends like Bob Lombard, Fritz, Burrhead and even hire on some "wetbacks" once in a while. They would

1939 Onofre surf contest. {Left to right} Tuley Clark, Al Bixler, Don Okey, Bob Humphreys, Dorian Paskowitz, Lloyd Baker, Pete Peterson, Gard Chapin, Vincent "Klotz" Lindberg, Lorrin Harrison, winner of the Tom Blake Perpetual Trophy.

all help process or sometimes the guys would go out and dive too. It was a happy, hard working time. The sound of knives zinging on the steels, the rhythmic pounding, set the perfect accompaniment for story and song. The cats on the floor waited patiently for scraps from the pounding blocks. Babies slept in baskets as the zinging, singing, and pounding continued through the night.

Ginger and I liked to feel around in the guts for pearls. We could just feel them through the outside membrane, which we had to break when we found one. It was kind of a yucky mess. But they were beautiful. Not perfectly round and white like oyster pearls but free form in all shapes and colors. The total operation of processing the abs was clean

Lobster fishing with brother Fred in Lorrin's home-made skiff.

and efficient. After shucking and gutting, the shells were dumped in big ravines or over cliff edges. Probably now buried under freeways. There was a drain in the shop floor so that the whole place could be scrubbed and hosed down at the end of a working day.

In a few short years the babies joined us, Marian, Lorrin Jr., and Jennifer. We would all pile in the car on Fridays to deliver abalones up the coast to Santa Monica and down to Carlsbad. Stopping at the back of restaurants such as Victor Hugo's in Laguna, Daddy would enter into the kitchens and materialize with fancy pastries for us from the French chefs. Deliveries had to be on Friday 'cause Saturday and Sunday were reserved for surfing.

Above All, Have Fun

C H A P T E R   1 1

The barn felt cool to me on the hot summer day. I dug my bare toes through the soft layer of silt and sawdust to feel the hard floor underneath. It was just dirt but so hard it felt like cement. I remembered the first time I went into the barn. It contained an old horse-drawn buggy, cow hides hanging from the rafters and a warm milky smelling calf in the one stall.

That was when the Winterborns, Lele's relatives, lived in the house for a while with her. Now that she and my dad were married they had moved elsewhere, and the buggy had given way to saw horses, sandpaper, tools, varnish, redwood, assorted diving and fishing paraphernalia and projects in various stages.

Daddy subscribed to the school "If you can dream it, you can do it," or rather in his case, build it. His creations weren't necessarily for practical purposes. They were more inventive and he was compulsive about building them. When he was involved in a project not much could distract him.

As I approached him, the redwood shavings from his plane were curling and rolling to the floor. Not looking up he stated, "This is going to be the greatest. Have to take a little off the nose and dish this scoop out more." I sat quietly on a fish box beside him enjoying the clean fresh smell of the redwood. He rattled on nonstop talking more to himself than to me. "Don't know whether this will work or not

Lorrin's barn.

Swell day at 'Nofre.

but we'll try it." As the twelve-foot block of wood took on
a surfboard shape, it started looking more like a saucer. He
dug deeper into the deck, scooping it out, making it more
boat than board. "I had a dream the other night about this.
It might work. Hmmm! Hand me that sandpaper, Rosie."
He worked on until supper, then continued late into the
night to whittle and shave away. I sat and watched and
brought him tools he needed until my eyes would no
longer stay open. He sanded it and just put on one coat of
varnish because this was an invention and might not fly—
or, rather, surf. Several days later it went with us to San
Onofre where it did fail its test flight—just filled up with
water and was sluggish on a wave. I'm not sure what he did
with that redwood, probably used it for another project.
I don't remember seeing it propped against the walls with
the many other surfboards ranging in size from seven to

fifteen feet. Some were solid woods and others hollow or laminated, creating stripes of light and dark tones, giving the illusion of inlay.

I loved sitting in that old barn listening, watching, and assisting occasionally as he happily labored away. Often he was in such a hurry to get it in the water, he didn't put the finishing touches on too carefully. But having the fun of building it, testing it and, if it was successful, enjoying using it, was all important.

The boats, lobster traps, the shop and many of the items needed for commercial fishing, my dad built himself. But most of all he really liked to create just for the fun of it. Lots of the results were a quick fix, but then there was the thirty-eight-foot dugout outrigger. It took him five years to build it.

He had a dream. We drove back into the valley from San Onofre. He had looked at the old sycamore tree for a long time imagining how the natural bow in it would shape into the perfect surfing canoe much like the ancient Polynesian Koa wood outriggers. The 'Nofre gang accompanied us with saws, ropes, and chains, everyone ready to lend a hand to bring down the old sycamore for Lorrin.

The sunlight caught on the pale grey trunk with golden brown patches like age spots darkening on the face of a grand old lady. The tree was majestic and slightly leaned off at an angle. It took some doing to bring her down. Then she was revered, covered and cared for while curing for several years. Well, it should have been five years of curing but Lorrin was impatient to begin the work. On poor wave days at San Onofre, when they would rather be playing music, drinking beer and dancing, Daddy would heckle and prod, "Oh it will be fun to work on the canoe. We'll all be able to ride waves in it. Let's do it." Everyone did get to use the big sycamore canoe finally. They rode waves in it and dove out of it. Voss and Margret's daughter, Luana, remembers having to accompany her dad on skin-diving expeditions in the canoe because they could get an extra limit with her along. Sometimes she got pretty bored waiting for them.

They swamped it too in some mighty "hair-raising" surf. It was big, heavy and difficult to turn over and a few of us spent the rest of the time bailing water out with old buckets or coffee cans tied to the seats, while my dad maneuvered to catch another big wave.

I must have been ten when he finished it because I gave a report on it in the fifth grade. I might as well have been talking about a safari in outer Mongolia. None of the kids in my class could relate except for one boy. He was from an affluent family that had traveled to Hawaii several times and had ridden in outrigger canoes at Waikiki. Oh, was he ever my childhood sweetheart! Someone who could sort of understand my other life. Since I lived in Tustin with Grandma to go to school, I blocked out the beach life during the week. It's amazing that my dad and the beach were only thirty miles away and Tustin people had never seen a surfer, much less an outrigger, except in magazine ads for Hawaii. Well, Southern California was primarily an agricultural area until 1960 and most farmers didn't go to the beach. I say most 'cause my dad liked to farm too. After the old walnut trees were removed he planted and cultivated avocados.

As head of the household, he set the rules for us kids to live by: Absolutely no smoking, "Just nothing but a human incinerator." No cussing. (Ginger got her mouth washed out with soap. That cured me of ever even considering uttering an expletive.) A little beer or wine was okay. Work hard, love your fellow man, above all have fun, enjoy life and you had better be ready to load into the car at 9:00 a.m.

Lorrin's first surfing canoe made of planks.

Surfing outrigger at 'Nofre.

Summer day at San Onofre. Notice coffee-can sand buckets.

sharp on Saturday and Sunday morning to go to the beach. Have your bathing suit with you because he's not going back to get it. That happened to "Little Lorrin" so many times, he got used to wearing his trunks on his head so that he wouldn't forget them.

Speaking of bathing suits, my dad was sewing them for Ginger and me. We didn't have wet suits in those days. So he would haunt the Army/Navy stores for old woolen underwear, sweaters and uniforms. He cut black wool trunks for us out of sailor suits. They were laced on the sides with the heavy cotton cord used for fish line. Needless to say they probably weren't the most attractive beach wear for two little girls. Well, Ginger was almost nine years old and these suits didn't have a top. He insisted that she wear them and she was mortified. I thought they were wonderful. What if they did tend to get heavy with water and stretch out. I was constantly pulling them up. I think Lele took pity on us and finally bought us some real bathing suits. But Daddy could never see the point. "The wool is much better and warmer. They don't need those fancy things." Well, I have to agree that girls bathing suits in those days were not designed for surfing. They were either riding up our crotches or pulling on our necks, and they always filled up with sand. We spent a lot of time rolling up the beach in the shore breaks.

After a long Saturday at the beach and a hearty dinner, we would curl up on the floor in front of the big radio with the green glass eye that lit up and listen to Hawaii Calls. I fell asleep listening to the soft guitars and Hawaiian falsetto voices, the smell of lemon tingling my nostrils. My dad was big into lemons. He washed his hair with them, used them for mouth wash and for colds and sore throats. They were supposed to lighten and brighten your hair.

Sunday morning we would lie on the floor in front of

37

the radio and he would read us the funnies in the paper and laugh. They must have been funnier to him than they were to me. Then it was off to the beach for another day of surf, sand, sun, and seaweed. Ginger and I were delivered to Grandma's backdoor late Sunday evening so that we could go to school the next day.

I can't even imagine what we must have looked like to her, but I do remember more than once she stripped us down right there outside on her back porch before she took us in the house and popped us into the bath tub of her elegant bathroom. Grandma was a fanatic about neatness. I don't know how she tolerated us two rascally messy girls. Papa built her Spanish Mediterranean home in 1930. It had large rooms with tile everywhere and a big patio with wrought iron gates. One bathroom was huge. The walls were tiled in light blue and white with black trim and water lilies. The black tiles extended in an arch over the tub that was set into the wall, ceiling and all tiled in blue. After returning from my dad's for any length of time we were promptly sent there. If we weren't filled with seaweed and sand we were covered with dirt, abalone and fish goo sticking to our jeans and foxtails in our hair, our feet as black as tar babies on the bottom. Probably were packing fleas from the dog as well. I don't remember that she ever complained about it though.

It was a dark night. We could hear dogs barking and lights flashing in the distance. Turning off his flashlight Daddy whispered to us in an urgent hushed tone, "We had better get out of here." Lele grabbed my hand and we tried to run through the brambles of willows and poison oak. It seemed like I was airborne most of the way as I was being pulled along the rough winding path toward home,

Ginger tide-pooling at San Onofre.

The Richfield gas station tower was a landmark. The perfect take-off spot
was the lineup of the lifeguard tower and the Richfield sign.
With Hammerhead, Doheny, 1946.

39

"The Jungle." Looking across the valley toward Dana Point.
Lobster traps in middle ground.

twigs and nettles smarting as they snapped in my face.

The plan was to net steelhead salmon out of the San Juan Creek, "the river," as they swam upstream from the ocean. Apparently this practice was illegal. The lights we saw might have been the Fish and Game wardens. We couldn't take any chances. I believe they were the only people in the world that my dad didn't like. They continued a feud for years. Actually it was more like a "cat and mouse" game. He didn't go for them trying to control his business, always snooping on him and dictating what he could and could not do. The Fish 'n' Game, however, certainly didn't trust him an inch and seemed to have nothing better to do than antagonize him.

When we were fishing, Ginger and I were sure that they lurked behind every rock and bush on the cliffs above us. The unseen demons going by the names of Decker and Terwilliger were watching every move we made through binoculars. For some time I wasn't sure what Fish 'n' Game was, never actually having seen them.

Daddy carefully measured each lobster to make sure it was legal size, then threw the small ones back. He did the same with abalones, and never sold "shorts" to restaurants or fish buyers. But occasionally he sneaked a few "shorts" in for Grandma and Papa, not only because they asked for them but also just to spite Decker and Terwilliger, I think. I never could understand why Grandma and Papa preferred the small lobsters to the big ones. They claimed the meat was richer and more succulent. Restaurants seemed to gauge the quality of a lobster tail on its size.

After we came into the cove from fishing, Ginger was instructed to tie the boat to its moorings while Daddy conveniently made sure the gunny sack containing the "shorts" was attached under the side of a little skiff away from the view of the Fish 'n' Game. We carefully coiled ropes and stowed away gear before we rowed the skiff to shore, hoping all the while the bag would not float to the surface. The game plan was that if Decker and Terwilliger were watching they would not suspect anything was awry. Ginger continued to work at the bow of the skiff as Daddy, carefully holding the sack of shorts out of sight, and I pushed on the stern winching the boat up the beach.

The San Juan Creek, which we called The River, was probably not even a half mile behind our house and was usually no more than a trickle. But after spring rains it could get pretty swollen. Behind the barn the little dirt road followed beside the walnut grove to the railroad tracks. From there on was a jungle with a rough trail through it to the river.

Now we were racing along that seldom used trail in the middle of the night as if our lives depended on it. Lele clutched my hand and stifled a giggle as she tripped on rocks and exposed roots, pushing aside the dense growth. Ginger ran ahead carrying the flashlight and Daddy was behind bringing the net that wanted to tangle in the branches. I wasn't sure whether to be more frightened of the Fish 'n' Game or of falling in the jungle. I don't remember ever getting any steelhead. Trying to catch our breath it seemed a long way to run before we reached the safety of home. Lele made us all cups of hot chocolate and tried to soothe my fears.

Tarzan Slept In My Bed

C H A P T E R   I I I

Most of the walnut groves of California had long since given way to orange trees. The latest agricultural enterprise was avocados. We still enjoyed the shade of the gnarled old walnut trees as we picked the nuts encased in their green shell until our fingers turned black. They cured on long racks on the hillside behind the barn, the green husks turning dark and dry in the sun.

Caesar, the old Mexican, farmed the field next to us with a mule and hand plow. It wasn't too uncommon in the '40s to see horse-drawn wagons and farm equipment still in use.

One day my dad came walking home from the river leading a bay stallion. His name was Bill. He was fairly gentle for a stallion. I had absolutely no fear of horses and was always climbing up the boards of the stall in the barn to pet his nose or give him a clump of green grass.

When Daddy tossed me up on top of the big horse I was sure I was in heaven. Something must have spooked him or else he was just feeling his oats. He took off under the walnut trees at a full gallop. I could hear voices yelling to hang on. I clung to his mane and flattened my body close to his as we raced under the low branches, lead rope flying behind. When he took a sharp turn I flew in one direction while he stopped abruptly in the other, everyone rushing to grab him and me. Except for the wind being knocked out of me, I thought it was pretty fun. Horseback

43

riding was the same concept as surfing to me. You didn't go without falling. It was part of the package. I hardly ever remember a day without falling. I learned to do it well.

Bill was probably a lot more ornery than I suspected. Stallions generally do not make the best family pets. Out in the field he reared up and came down on a tree stump tearing the soft fleshy part of his chest wide open. Daddy led him into the barn, cleansed the wound, and plastered it with gooey, black 3M glue. It worked perfect, healing almost as good as new with very little scarring.

When it was finally decided Bill was too much horse for us, he was traded for Tony, a small blue roan. Tony ran over the railroad track and injured himself so badly that he had to be put down.

Then came Talent. Talent was a two-year-old bay gelding with a nonchalant attitude and a calm disposition. As far as I could see his only talent lay in finding any patch of green grass and heading for it at a run. All of us kids got to enjoy him. He lived to be twenty-eight years old. You really have to give him credit for that. He certainly was rarely pampered. Some winters he had little to eat but tree bark and bamboo. He did have a talent for survival and was amazingly healthy. In the pasture on the other side of the railroad tracks he became slick and fat in the summer months.

We bought a saddle on a trip to Tijuana where "Little Lorrin" wandered off and was lost for a while. He was two years old, towheaded and carrying one of those woven straw horses. Lele frantically tried to converse in Spanish to vendors and street people describing the lost little boy. Very soon we found him heading around a corner clutching the souvenir straw horse to his chest, his eyes wide with fear.

The saddle seemed stiff and we were all so used to riding bareback that we didn't use it often. It must have

Marian on Talent, our beach horse. He lived to be 28 years old.

Family trip to Tijuana to buy a saddle.

Looking from the hill toward Capistrano Beach, 1952.

been made for a three-hundred-pound person. It was so big none of us kids could lift it onto Talent's back.

The jungle between the railroad tracks and the river had been cleared, but the bamboo and shrubbery grew back quickly. The river was bulldozed and left to wander open sandy areas for many years before steep concrete walls for flood control were erected.

Talent loved to run in the river bed. He also loved to roll in it saddle off or on. We never broke him of this habit and we knew we better be prepared to jump off when his knees started buckling. Sometimes we'd have three on board and we would all go flying in every direction as he went down closing his eyes in ecstasy as he rolled back and forth in the sand.

As long as Talent was munching on grass or bamboo he was oblivious to us kids. We could climb up his neck and slide down his tail and he didn't seem too concerned.

In my teens I would ride him bareback down the river to Doheny where we would run along the beach, splashing in the shore break. Sometimes I would leave early in the morning and ride up to Hobie's in Dana Point to see Phil Edwards. He was working there shaping surfboards. He would jump up behind me on Talent and we would ride out to the point and look over the cliff to check out the lines of surf. If it was good waves we would go surfing for the day. If it was flat we'd work.

Much later I brought an old Arabian mare, Raja, to live with Talent. Raja had a multitude of ailments mostly due to old age. I thought they would be good company. She had lived a gentler life, however, and didn't forage well in the pasture on Talent's roughage diet.

When she injured her leg, my dad rigged up a sling on a pulley that he attached to a tree over a low ravine. He suspended her in it, fed her every day and she seemed to be recovering until the rope broke. She fell, breaking her neck. Daddy was visually distraught. There was nothing left to do but bury her right there. That task accomplished, he felt somewhat relieved. The next day he went back to check on her and all four feet had popped straight out of the ground. Alarmed, he pushed them back in and covered them up again. When they popped out again the coyotes and varmints were getting to them so he covered her with chicken wire and more dirt. There Raja rests in peace today probably with a new highway over the top of her.

Talent only lived a short time after. For twenty-six of his twenty-eight years he had been a part of our family. Lele didn't want him to have to suffer Raja's fate. So, Daddy and Fly—Jean Pierre Van Swae, AKA "The Fly"— loaded the dead horse on a trailer, threw a carpet over him and proceeded to the dump. Now, it was illegal to bury horses in California. I'm certain dumping them at the local landfill was frowned upon. It was tricky unloading him between the earth movers. Trying to keep him covered with the carpet they slid him off the trailer as inconspicuously as possible and quickly left the scene.

Lorrin Harrison definitely was a family man. He just went about it in different ways. Loving to see us kids have fun, he made us many things to play with. Of course, he wanted to see us have fun surfing more than anything else, so he built us our own surfboards. The first ones were truly works of art. They were made of pine and redwood. The redwood edged the little boards and was mitered to form an upside down "V" on the nose. Mine was three and one half feet long and Ginger's was four feet. Our names were beautifully decaled on the decks. They sported many coats of varnish each sanded carefully before the next one was applied then rosined off to glow like a fine piece of furniture. And they were heavy. Almost

Rosie stylin'. 'Nofre, 1945.

The Shack.

as wide as a big board they were too wide for us to carry
and almost too wide for us to paddle. It was all I could do
to drag mine down to the water at six years old, much less
carry it. They didn't catch waves very well either unless
Daddy came out and shoved us, but we had fun paddling
them around and floating over swells.

One day I brought mine in where I had drifted down
by "Dog Patch." No one was down the beach that far to
help me bring it up. They were all up at the shack.

The San Onofre shack was a gathering place built of
poles roofed and sealed with palm tree limbs. It was ever
changing. Some years it had walls, sometimes just a roof,
and once it had an added-on palm-lined fence. Boards

The gang at 'Nofre.

always leaned against it. It provided protection from wind and sun. It still stands today.

So I left my little board on the wet sand and promptly forgot about it as I went to join the group at the shack. The tide came up and we never saw that great little board again. Wouldn't I love to have it today. I'm not sure what eventually happened to Ginger's. She says Daddy sold it.

When balsa became popular Daddy made three little potato chip boards for Marian, Lorrin, and Jennie. They were pure white with small pieces of abalone shell inlaid in the deck. The shell was cut into initials. Jennie's had a small coconut shell J. These became known as the M. board, L. board, and J. board. Being very thin and light

*Daddy made lots of toys for us. The wagon shafts are boat oars.
Lorrin Jr, Jip the dog, cousins and Marian, center.*

weight the kids could carry them and they caught and
rode waves beautifully. Over the years he made more
boards for them that included starfish, horn shark horns,
carved coconut shells, and abalones under the fiber glass.

He built other things for us too. We had fun walking
on the stilts he made us out of 2x4's. He tried to teach us
how to use slings that he made like the kind David slew
Goliath with. Ginger recalls slinging mudballs at a garage
for practice. They stuck on the white siding like swallows
nests. I could never master the art, usually losing a rock
out the back on the first swing.

It was fun to slide down the hill on tin sleds, cardboard,
or whatever he found for us. The tin sleds had rolled edges

because we got cut a few times before we discovered the raw edges were dangerous. I did as much rolling down the hill through the cockleburs and foxtails as I did sliding.

The wagon had shafts made for it out of boat oars so that we could hitch Jip, our shepherd, to it to pull us. At Christmas we received gifts of mother of pearl cut into tiny hearts on gold chains or little pendants. There was never a lot of money. We didn't have expensive toys. But the lesson was to make do with what there was, and "if you can build it, why buy it."

I was named after the song "Rose Marie I Love You," that played on an old music box. He made me a case out of a red abalone shell to set it in. Ginger was named after the Ginger flower of Hawaii. Our dad impressed on us dreams of paradise and to him that was Hawaii. He never wanted to live or work there, but he always wanted to go back for a vacation. It became his goal to take us all with him.

The old adobe is now on the historical register. Having been built by the local Indians before the San Juan Capistrano Mission, Henry Dana supposedly used it as a trading post for hides. Another theory is that it was the early mission. The walls are three feet thick. Actually they are two walls of adobe bricks with an air space in between.

When we first came to live there with Cecelia the outer walls were exposed. Ginger and I could dream up all kinds of stories to go with the hand prints and straw in the big mud blocks. We didn't get to go into the attic often but it contained wonderful things. We discovered an old Spanish cape like Zorro's, a silver mounted bit with delicate chains and trunks containing antique clocks and music boxes. These provided ideas for our games. We played cowboys and horses and Spanish vaqueros. Ginger was pretty creative. She made braided bridles for us with bits made out of bathtub chains to hold in our teeth.

In the middle of the night small varmints would find ways to get into the inner walls of the adobe. I'm positive they had a network throughout that they began building when the house was first constructed. Many nights I lay in my bed too afraid to go to sleep, conjuring up monsters in my mind as I listened to little feet running and scratching through the walls. It was very cold in the winter except in the living room by the fireplace. Until Lele bought us electric blankets I remember curling into a ball and freezing all night.

Daddy was always hot and liked windows open even in the winter months. He said it was because he spent so much time diving in cold water that he was used to it.

The house and barn have not changed much. In 1949 they plastered over the adobe. That was the demise of the little animals scurrying through the walls. Rain water draining from the hill behind was eroding one corner of the house. They also remodeled and added on a kitchen with a big picture window looking out over the field. At the other end a bedroom and bath were added.

The field and property surrounding them has given way to progress but the house and barn remain the same. While visiting, my granddaughter mentioned, "I like the way Grandma Lele's house feels." People from all walks of life love to visit and gather at the house. My dad entertained doctors, lawyers, movie stars, and bums. I liked to say "Tarzan slept in my bed." Johnny Weismuller occasionally visited us on his way to a swim competition and he really did spend the night in my bed. I slept on the couch.

It wasn't unusual to see stars like Betty Grable, Arthur Lake, or Jackie Coogan at San Onofre. They liked to get

View of the "hide house" circa 1940. Cecelia inherited the adobe from her grandmother, Theresa Yorba, who inherited the property from her mother, Rosa Avila, who received it as a wedding present from her father, Juan Avila.

Lorrin did some remodeling on the house in 1949.
The adobe bricks shown were handmade by Lorrin.

Whitey and Matt Brown tandem at Corona del Mar.

away from the Hollywood hubbub. Betty Grable didn't like it though. She sat on the beach impatient to leave. Richard Jaekel and Jim Arness became regulars at the beach. Daddy taught several celebrities to surf, Buddy Ebsen being one. He played stand-in parts in a few movies now and then also.

When Marian was a baby he took her tandem in a Pete Smith film short. I was asked to be in one with another famous surfer, Pete Peterson, and his wife. I was nine years old. We were trying to perform a three high trandem. It was a fun weekend. They took me for a ride in a helicopter and paid me $50, which was like a million to me. The waves were never big enough for us to be successful that weekend. Pete did get us both up, me on

56

Surfing tandem with Muriel at Queens, Waikiki, 1935.

her shoulders and her on his several times but by then the wave would be dying out. That film never made it but I used to see Marian and my dad surfing on that Pete Smith film into the fifties when I was going on dates to the drive-in movies.

Fishing is hard on hands. Even though my dad wore cotton gloves, most of the time his hands and lower arms looked as though they were covered with barnacles. Cuts and abrasions caused by sharp fins, claws, and wire became easily infected from poisons toxic to the skin. Walking barefoot on rocks at low tide, he always managed to sustain a few minor abrasions. He paid little attention to small discomforts. Tough and crusty, he often resembled the creatures he took from the sea.

It was very seldom that he was ever sick. However, the spring after our mother died, he came limping into Grandma's yard. He had stepped on a nail, chose to ignore it and it had begun to fester. His leg looked like a blimp by the time he walked the ten miles from Costa Mesa to Tustin. Blood poisoning had set in. He needed help. The doctor administered the necessary antibiotics and ordered him to stay in bed for two weeks. Ginger and I were delighted to have him in the big bed in Grandma's guest room. He didn't stay there for too long though.

Knocking toenails off with fish boxes, cutting hands while trimming abs, getting conked on the head with surf boards were just the daily routine of work and play, but he seemed to instinctively know when it was absolutely necessary to seek medical attention.

During the '70s Jennie and her family lived in a little house on the other side of the railroad tracks. They were always getting poison oak. Jen had it and no one was too concerned until she came up to the house one day looking like puffed wheat, her eyes completely shut. Daddy demanded, "Get her to the hospital NOW!"

Several summers ago he and I and my grandson, Brandon, went surfing at 'Nofre for the day. It was nice little waves. Brandon stayed inside catching soups while we were farther out. We saw his board pearl and spin up into the air. When we caught some waves and came in Brandon said his board hit him on the head. He had a nice big slice on his head washed clean by the salt water. I didn't want to panic and frighten Brandon, but I was really concerned as my dad stood around the fire ring warming his hands and visiting with a couple from Costa Rica. We ate their burritos and

1932, working as a loader for Olive Heights Citrus Assoc.

Harrison family at Doho.

Coaching the team.

dried by the fire until we were ready to go. Then Grandpa
Lorrin turned to Brandon and remarked off-handedly,
"Guess we had better get you to the hospital now for stitches."

The '36 Ford had about seen its last day. Ginger fell
out of those old suicide doors more than once when
we were going around corners. It was about to rust
away from salt water. We just had a jeep pickup for awhile.
The little kids rode in front, Ginger and I in the back in
sleeping bags and blankets in the winter and on fish boxes,
lobster traps and surfboards in the summer. Sometimes it
was freezing, but I never remember complaining—wasn't
the thing to do.

Daddy rigged up a sort of tent camper for the back
and took us all to Big Bear to play in the snow one winter.
Overnight we had a big storm and were snowed in for a
few days. We thought it great fun but he wasn't too happy
until he was able to get back home to the beach. After
that snowstorms and cold country always made him
feel insecure.

I always thought he should do an ad for Quaker Oats.
He started almost every morning with a huge bowl of
oatmeal followed by pancakes or bacon, eggs and toast.
I was so tuned out by oatmeal I could hardly look at a
bowl of mush much less eat it when I was a kid. He always
made sure I got a few bites down before we made our trek
to the sea.

Cecelia was a mastermind at saving money, but there
was always plenty of food even in tough times and she was
a great cook. We enjoyed her homemade tortillas as a
special treat and chorizo con huevos. She kept a garden and
during the summer we had lots of fresh vegetables to enjoy
with our regular ration of lobster, abalone, and fish.

After spending a day on the ocean appetites tended to flourish. A peanut butter and jam sandwich tasted as good as a T-bone steak. At San Onofre we had a loaf or two of bread, peanut butter, jam, lunch meat, and lettuce. If you stayed out surfing too long the meat and jam were always gone. I learned to love peanut butter and lettuce sandwiches.

Homemade jam every year was a must. A day was spent going to Santa Ana to pick strawberries, boysenberries, or apricots. We ate as many as we picked. Ginger and I considered the whole process a great delight. The best part was when the bubbly stuff was skimmed off the top of the jam boiling in the pot and we were allowed small bowls of the frothy stuff to eat.

For a small person my dad could amazingly pack the food away. He had such a high energy level, he literally burned it off as fast as he ate it. My grandmother said she had never met anyone that could eat as much as Lorrin, "He ate a whole loaf of bread at one time." Actually that was not unusual for all the guys in my family. They seemed to devour whatever was put on the table in front of them.

Clearing the field on a hot, dry day, he spotted what looked like horseradish. After digging the root out he brushed it off a little and popped it in his mouth. It had an unusual succulent taste. He decided after a few chews that it wasn't horseradish and spit it out promptly forgetting about it. As he approached the house he started feeling strange. He wanted water and drank and drank then threw the glass out the back door. A stack of diapers looked like they had gremlins crawling out of them. Gooey stuff ran down the walls. Rainbows of color moved around him like a kaleidoscope. His behavior was so erratic Cecelia called the doctor. Believing he was suffering sun stroke when they arrived, the doctor and nurse could see his eyes were dilated

Rosie and Ginger, San Onofre, winter 1945.

but didn't have a clue as to what was the cause. They gave him a sedative that did little to help the situation then left. He was sure the nurse had a bloody nose. It was so frightening to Cecelia she hardly slept all night. The next day they discovered the root that he had chewed on was jimson weed, a toxic plant which causes hallucinations and death. He was lucky to be alive.

Holidays were always so much fun. Cecelia cooked turkey for Thanksgiving stuffed with a wonderful dressing.

64

The recipe had been passed down in the Yorba family. It was rich with raisins, sausage, and olives in true Spanish tradition. We always ate until we were stuffed. Then my dad said we had to run around the house four times before we came in to play games or take a siesta.

The day before Christmas we made cookies and pies. Ginger and I excitedly helped prepare dinner for the next day and stuff the stockings for the three little kids. Cecelia hand knitted the large stockings for all of us, often working long into the nights to have them done by Christmas. Each one had a different design according to what color yarn she had available. They were mostly filled with nuts, oranges, and apples with a few toys and articles in between. We thought all seven of them looked wonderful hanging over the big brick fireplace on the redwood mantle.

"Pop" Proctor came over to play Santa Claus and give us candy. After the little guys went to bed he stayed to watch us put the presents under the tree and we had cocoa. Pop never drank any because he didn't believe in drinking milk, so he would indulge in a glass of wine instead.

The Christmas tree sometimes was a real pine tree. Other years it might have been tumble weeds or a century plant. The century plant Christmas tree was really beautiful and unusual.

Paradise

C H A P T E R I V

In 1953 Lorrin was to realize his dream of taking the entire family to Hawaii. He had a good year fishing lobsters and diving for abs in '52. They were able to save enough to take us on the S.S. Lurline, the Matson luxury ocean liner.

As I stood at the train station in Santa Ana, wearing my new skirt and blouse, I could hardly believe I was really going to spend two whole months out of school, ten days on the boat and six weeks in the land that had been proclaimed as paradise for as long as I could remember.

Grandma had packed two small suitcases and an overnight case for Ginger and me. They contained one dress, several shorts, shirts, and underwear. We would have to buy new bathing suits there because they were not available in California in January and we had outgrown and worn out the ones from the previous summer.

Ginger and I had butterflies in our stomachs as we boarded the Starlight with the rest of the family. I had never been on a train before. We had to travel from Santa Ana to San Francisco to catch the Lurline. Ginger was fifteen, I was twelve and one half, Marian, Lorrin and Jennie almost six, four and two. They would celebrate their birthdays over there. We were so wound up I don't think we slept much on the overnight ride.

Daddy had made four brand new balsa wood boards to take with us. They were the latest thing and lightweight enough that we could carry them. He could hardly wait

Waikiki Beach.

for us to try them out in the tropic waters of Hawaii. Five kids, four boards, guitar, uke, diving gear, and luggage was plenty to pack along. Never having been on a cruise ship as a paying passenger before, he was eagerly looking forward to the five-day trip to the islands.

On the chilly morning in January we took a taxi through the old section of Frisco to the Matson line docks to board the Lurline. None of us had ever ridden in a taxi. We scrunched most of us in the back seat with Daddy and one of the kids on his lap in front, and off we went. As soon as the taxi driver found out where we were from and where we were going, he really got into the spirit of the ride. He took us whizzing up and down hills, through the center of downtown San Francisco. After we recovered our stomachs a few times, we decided this was great fun. The driver shouted out our story to some of his peers along the way and we shouted and laughed too. Aside from feeling a little weak-kneed when we finally arrived at the docks, we all managed to board the Lurline on time. The band played "Aloha Oe" as the grand ship left the harbor and glided under the Golden Gate Bridge.

The huge ship rocked and rolled slowly on the sea feeling a lot like being in an elevator that rocked sideways as well as up and down. Cecelia didn't feel well most of the five days. Since the dinners and meals were part of the ticket price we could order anything on the menu that we wanted. Ginger and I thought it was all free. They offered extensive choices of appetizers, soups, salads, buffet, four or five entrees and accompaniments, and of course a delightful variety of desserts. I wasn't necessarily interested in gourmet food at my age, but Dad loved it. He ate two goose dinners, pheasant under glass, steak and the elegant desserts with all the trimmings.

The S.S. Lurline was touted as being 632 feet in length, 79 feet across, with a gross tonnage of 18,500, air-conditioned throughout and accommodating 722 passengers, all in first class. It was like a small city to us and there was always something going on. We did spend a lot of time just walking around gawking at things. We took the hula lessons along with what seemed to be all elderly wealthy ladies. We learned "The Hukilau" and went to the Ho'omalimali, a party with games designed for the tourists, Malihinis. I'm not sure how they reacted to us kids invading their realm doing the hula and winning the prizes. Ginger and I were so prepped for this trip. Not only had we listened, talked, sang Hawaii all of our lives, we digested everything written about the islands that was available to us. We devoured the Armine von Tempski books, *Pam's Paradise Ranch* (I must have read it at least five times) and *Born in Paradise.*

Ginger won first place in the Hula Contest aboard the Lurline.

Aboard ship there were lots of orientation films to watch about pineapple and sugar cane. We were both "A" students and we brought our school workbooks with us and would send papers home as we did them. We didn't do much homework on the boat though. Too many interesting events taking place! Ping pong, paddle tennis, swimming, dancing, movies, games. We tried to take in as much as our ages would allow, never having been exposed to this world before. We had both taken dancing class for several years—tap, ballet, and toe—so hula was pretty easy for us, and the older people were amazed at our proficiency and grace, especially Ginger. She was really into her dancing. The instructor discovered her talents and put her in front of the group more than once. She danced in the talent show and received a gift.

Classic photo, Ethel Kukea surfing at Waikiki.

Entering the enormous dining room the night of the Captain's dinner, we weren't prepared for the elaborate decorations, balloons and streamers. The ladies were all dressed in long formal gowns and the men in tuxedos. We weren't. Daddy, of course was wearing his best aloha shirt, slacks, and real shoes. I had never seen my dad wear real shoes as much as he did that five days. We were not aware that this was the waning of a glamorous period in time. When jet airliners made their debut it was the death of the two Matson Liners to Hawaii in the late 1950s. With the advent of *Love Boat* in the '70s, credit and inflation, cruise ships became popular for everyone, but they never brought back the S.S. Lurline and Matsonia with their '30s and '40s gracious luxury. We enjoyed the squab dinner close

Bon Voyage. 1935.

to the captain's table, but I think we were more entranced by the formality and surroundings than we were the five-course meal.

Standing on the deck in the ghost of dawn, the emerald green islands were a breathtaking sight as they began to appear in our view. As we rounded Diamond Head we could see the coastal aqua blue waters and Honolulu. It was a magic moment in time. The native boys were diving for coins that people threw around the ship when we came into port. Daddy told us how he did that with them before just for fun. Polynesian girls wearing real ti leaf hula skirts swayed gracefully to the music of a band. The pungent smell of plumerias, jasmine, ginger, and pikaki drifted to our nostrils on the light tropical breeze as Uncle Joe and

Aunt Ethel placed the traditional flower leis around our necks and hugged and kissed us.

Joe and Ethel were always a part of the mystique of the islands for us. We had only seen either of them briefly a few times in our lives in California, but the stories of Hawaii always included Joe and Ethel. Joe Kukea is full-blooded Hawaiian directly descended from royal family. He and Ethel were pen pals in the '30s. It was popular to have a pen pal those years. It was at the same time that she and Lorrin were surfing at Corona Del Mar, California.

When my dad made his first stowaway trips to Oahu he looked up Joe and insisted if he ever got to the mainland to come see them and go surfing. Joe did come to California with the Honolulu fire department. After he and Ethel had corresponded so many years it was as though they were in love almost before they actually met. To her parents Hawaii must have seemed a far off land. I'm not sure that her mother ever forgave her for running away to marry Joe. But, I can't imagine two people more beautifully suited to each other.

Joe was tall and dark, with a sober, almost regal manner, he looked like he stepped right out of a Polynesian movie as a Kahuna. His voice echoed that ancient Hawaiian mellowness and he seemed very focused on his goals in life. A hug from him was wonderfully warm and filled with significance.

Ethel was a big, strong, athletic woman with the kindest sun-etched face and big smile to match. She won the Woman's National Surfing Championships several years in a row. She taught a physical fitness class at the YWCA and Joe was captain of the Honolulu Fire Department. They had three beautiful hapa haole children, Kala, Kahele, and Mele, and were devoted, loving parents.

Houses in Hawaii are often built up on poles. Theirs was no exception. It made a garage and open-air basement

Joe and Kala Kukea, part of our ohana.

Rosie in tailor-made Linns bathing suit, Kuhio.

First day at Waikiki.

underneath. They lived in a primarily Hawaiian section of the slope behind Punchbowl Crater. After stopping there briefly to deposit our luggage we made our way wiki wiki to the beach, as quickly as possible.

The sands of Waikiki, clear warm water, and brightly colored coral—this was the beach our dreams were made of. Kuhio, the little area at the south end of the beach, was to become our favorite spot.

We were such an unusual phenomenon. "Family of seven travels to Hawaii with four surf boards, fins, and diving gear." A lady reporter came to take our pictures for the newspaper and interview us. We quickly made a trip to Sears to buy bathing suits for the photos. Mine was a one-piece brown tapa cloth print with all that elastic gathering and a pake shirt to match with real coconut shell buttons.

Later we would go to Linns to have tailor made suits for all of us. Linns trunks and bathing suits were sought after by surfers. They were made out of a soft but heavy royal blue denim and sported red and white trim down the sides like racing stripes. The Beachboys had worn them for years. They also made palaka trunks, a traditional Hawaiian plaid. The women's were two-piece and buttoned at each side in the front like sailor pants. They fit perfect and were great for surfing.

That first day we got our pictures taken for the paper, we were like real malahinis from the mainland in our tourist swimsuits and winter white skin. Everyone who was anyone in our book seemed to know Lorrin Harrison. As we walked down the beach it was, "Hey, Whitey, how you been? What's you doin' Bruddah? Long time no see."

We were introduced to Duke Kahanamoku and sat in the shade of the Outrigger Club and visited with him for a while. We met Rabbit Kekai, Blackout, Blue Makua, Splash, Steamboat, Pua, Yoyo, Curley, Mango, 8 Ball,

Nigger, Opu, Nose, Red, and even some with normal names like Barney, Johnny and Clarence. Our dad was literally treated as a celebrity of the famous Waikiki beach. This was especially exciting to Ginger who was going through the teenage "Father is not God" syndrome. Here it almost seemed like he was. So much camaraderie, laughing, joking! I think those guys talked as much with their hands as their voices. It was just as well too. Not being used to the heavy fluid pidgin, I would not have been able to understand them if they didn't sign everything they said with hands and body language.

With all of this fun going on, as soon as we got there, Daddy was making plans to build Ethel and Joe a diving skiff and balsa boards.

Johnny Ernstberg was one of the top beachboys. He and my dad had established a close friendship when they were batching together in the '30s. Johnny was a quiet man and Daddy seemed to enjoy coaxing a smile out of him. Dark tan and muscular, he was an excellent life guard, canoeman, and musician. He took us all surfing in his outrigger the second day we were there. We caught some dandy little waves off "Canoes." Canoes is the slower break at Waikiki used by the outriggers. Queens is the faster break for the surfers.

After a good ride, Jennie who was almost two said, "Do 'gain."

We thought we'd try Queens. There weren't too many surfers out. The waves were fun and fast, but it was easy to pearl and swamp the canoe. Jennie yelled "pull dive!" each time.

Duke

Kahele and Ginger with the "Chuck-a-luck."

"Papa he'e nalu!" The surf was up on the north shore! We needed wheels to travel to Makaha. We couldn't expect to use Joe and Ethel's car the whole two months we were there, so Daddy bought a 1936 Chevy sedan for $60. It was perfect. He could hardly wait to drill holes through the roof to install home-made surfboard racks on top. Kahele ran to the house shouting "It has pukas in the floor and Uncle Lorrin is making pukas in the top." The floorboards were so rusty they were eaten through in spots, leaving holes as big as three inches. We thought it was great fun to look down and see the road going by. What was left of the headliner hung in tatters, the old mohair upholstery faded and worn, but it was roomy and the seats were all there. Ethel christened it "the Chuck-a-luck."

"Rabbit" Kekai.

Makaha was a curved stretch of beach carved away by the big waves it was just beginning to become known for. We were only a little surprised to see a small group of San Onofre boys already camped there—Burrhead, Buzzy Trent, Walt and Flippy Hoffman along with Rabbit Kekai. On the way there Daddy pushed a stalled car for some local Hawaiian boys from Nanakuli and Waianae. They were so grateful, all ten of them helped set up our Army tent. Laughing and jabbering in pidgin English, they had it up in no time at all and we didn't have to do a thing.

Then it was out in the big waves. Man, those kids could surf! It seemed on just about anything. At Waikiki the Hawaiian beachboys were skilled with paddle boards. It was amazing to me that anyone could handle those big,

Makaha, 20' waves, 1953.

Johnnie, beachboy, Jennie and Marian, Kuhio.

heavy, hollow boxes. But at Makaha and in big surf, solid redwoods were popular. Balsa was still difficult to get in the islands, but it was starting to appear. The locals had redwoods or whatever scraps they could salvage and patch together to make a board. The style was long and narrow.

The steep beach front cut away by the sea caused a back wash and undertow. It was fascinating to watch the guys jump on their boards and catch the current out and get flipped when they hit the breakers. Most of the time the big waves didn't break all the way across creating a beautiful right slide. The depth and force of these waves were phenomenal. We suspected the lovely stretch of sand was destined to become famous someday. We didn't realize then just how much.

Lorrin was in his element. Shouting "Whoo Hoo!" after he dropped into a twenty-foot wall, he shot right across it like a speeding bullet in his inimitable style, the enormous wave folding gracefully behind him in a huge curl.

The heavy surf and rip tides kept us kids on the beach most of the time, but I don't ever remember being bored. We were confirmed wave watchers. Every break, every swell, every ride was a part of our training. We watched, learned and understood the ever changing surf for hours, days, weeks, years. It was exciting just to watch the guys make it through the big breaks or have some incredible wipeouts, big, heavy boards spinning sometimes thirty feet in the air. No bungy cords back then, they had to head for the coral when they lost it and stay low. We whooped and hollered and cheered for each one.

Daddy was so stoked. He was into speed and was especially interested in the boards they were using. George Downing called them "hot curl boards," the first big guns. We went to see him and checked out his design. The boards were long and narrow, pointed at the nose, narrower at the tail with a deep skeg. Rabbit could make his talk. When we got back to Joe and Ethel's, Daddy set right to the task of making his tandem board into a hot curl with a tail about six inches wide.

There were no facilities at Makaha. There was an outlet for water across the road, so we were able to haul it to our tent. The long crescent-shaped beach was lined with Kiawe trees and thorns—big thorns that made walking back into the trees to go shi shi difficult. Come to think of it, San Onofre didn't even have outhouses then. The canyon was the relief station, nicknamed Kukai Canyon.

Back at Waikiki the trade winds blew gently as we spent days getting bronzed by the sun and honing our surfing skills. With the new balsa boards that we could carry and handle on our own, Lele, Ginger and I were really surfing all by ourselves. Of course Daddy felt that he should coach our every move and we played around a lot. We started in Canoes, but soon advanced to Queens.

The beachboys had fun taking us tandem or out in their canoes when they weren't busy with a paying customer. The lady tourists were smart. They went tandem, which made them look good, but the guys usually rented boards and would tackle it on their own. We couldn't help laughing at their inability just to stay on the board, much less paddle it. The days went by as we soaked up the sun and surf and cut our feet on coral. The three little kids were swimming like fish in the clear warm water.

We had to do some real talking to convince Joe and Ethel to go to Makaha with us. I imagine living his whole life on an island, to Joe thirty miles seemed a long distance to travel. He definitely could not justify it just to go surfing. The waves were about eight feet—too big for us kids for surfing. We had fun swimming and body surfing in the shore breaks. If we got rained out we'd go home. Our dad

Whoo-hoo!!!

would work on a board or the boat and we would do our
studies. Almost every day we had at least one gentle rain
shower. It was usually a refreshing break from the intense
sun. I thought it was great when it rained while I was surfing, leaving rainbows afterwards.

Ginger, Lele, and I took hula lessons from a pretty
Hawaiian girl named Bunny. We learned quickly and it
was fun. I seriously question that her style was particularly
traditional by today's standards. Ethel made sure we were
exposed to a little of the Hawaiian culture other than surfing.
We went to Nuuanu Pali and Punchbowl. Ginger stayed
with Joe and Ethel several times when the rest of us made
the trek to the north shore. She visited the Bishop Museum,
the fire station, hula shows, and other cultural sights. I was
into the beach.

We became familiar faces at Makaha. A local welcoming
committee was usually on hand to greet us. Ginger and I
slept outside the tent on cots. It was wonderful to wake up
to the island sunrise and the rumble of the surf.

We went to an open-air theater in Waianae and sat on benches outside to watch the movie. If it rained hard we had to make a run for it and get a rain check.

Daddy was almost always successful spear fishing and we had excellent fish dinners. We watched the locals dive for wana (pronounced vana) sea urchins, open them on the beach and eat them raw. They were nasty to step on and broke off in our feet. We spent some evenings at home digging sea urchins out of Daddy's feet.

Riding Big Mamoo.

I felt so privileged to accompany the adults to the Edgewater Hotel where Johnny played guitar and sang with two other musicians. We sat in the open-air lounge by the sea often until midnight drifting and dreaming with the gentle flow of the Hawaiian melodies. My dad especially loved the way they played slack-key guitar and the falsetto voices. Afterward we would go to a little Chinese restaurant for a bowl of saimin or won ton min or noodle soups. Once we had pipi kaula poi, a salty, dried beef dipped in poi, Hawaiian cuisine. My palate was not always in tune with their delicacies. I nearly gagged one morning when I woke up to the most horrendous odor coming from the kitchen. Joe was cooking Hom Hii, stink fish, and eggs. He claimed it was delicious. I did enjoy the fresh bananas, pineapples, papayas, and other tropical fruits. We learned to make teriyaki, open coconuts, drink the sweet milk and eat the white meat. At Waikiki they had plate lunches of wonderful teriyaki, white rice, and salad for 50¢.

Joe and Ethel went to Kuhio with us to surf quite often. Joe was a good spear fisherman. He and the boys and Daddy would always bring in a nice bunch of fish for dinner.

When it rained almost every day we would take shelter under our boards leaning against the old tavern wall. There never seemed to be a dull moment with all the beachboys around offering us canoe rides, tandems, playing volleyball, or just clowning around entertaining us with their singing and joking. They taught Ginger and me how to stand on their shoulders, heads, and knees as we rode the waves tandem with them at Waikiki.

Many evenings one or two would come home with us and play and sing until early morning. Daddy literally attacked a ukulele. Banging away at it he strummed out all of the old tunes we knew by heart. Most of them were made famous by Harry Owens such as "Cockeyed Mayor of Kane Kakai," "Princess Pupuli Has Plenty Papaya," "Poi My Boy Will Make a Man of You." We laughed and sang along with these and dozens more like them. The Hawaiians had a soft gentle way of playing a uke and we learned some very old traditional songs from them like "Koni Au" and "Kaimana-Hila" all sung in Hawaiian. Joe, Kala, and Kahele were beautiful to watch together, blending the sounds of their Hawaiian ukuleles.

Poi My Boy

There's a south sea island staff of life
that makes the native laugh at life.
Oh! Fish and Poi daily diet
Boy oh boy you ought to try it.
Comes the starlight above and
I'm hungry for love
but the girl of my dreams is indifferent it seems.
Eat Poi every morning poi every evening
Poi my boy will make a man of you.
Comes the tropical rain and your sweety
complains of the night that intrans of
your lack of romance.
Eat Poi every morning poi every evening
Poi my boy will make a man of you.
Oh Kamehameha went to war with
nary a care. He never knew the meaning
of wear and tear. He waged a war
with all his might, fought all day and
he loved all night. There were
maidens galore and a thousand or more who
would line up and wait at his garden gate.
He ate poi every morning poi every evening
Poi my boy will make a man of you.
Oh you've heard about the mighty men of
Ho 'O Naunau they never touched a drop
of okolehau they're full of life at 93.
Why not you and why not me?
Oh believe every word of the story you've
heard about the hermits of old, you know
very well they ate Poi every morning
poi every evening
Poi my boy will make a man of you

87

Jammin'! Bob Jones, Bob, Murphy and Lorrin.

Their neighbor Jimmy Papa was married to a little Chinese lady that was an excellent seamstress. She even made her own patterns. My father always had her sew four or five silk Aloha shirts for him while he was there. My favorite was a soft grey with big red hibiscus flowers on it.

He made new coconut hats for all of us. Sitting on the beach weaving away, he learned a few new tricks from the beachboys. They would say, "Whitey, you make da kine like dis, is mo bettah kine fo you," and he would chuckle and crease the crown or leave flying ends to wave in the breeze. Each boy had his own style. It was such a treat for my dad to be able to weave with real coconut palm. In California he had to use the cocus palm that grew there. The yellow heart of that palm was pretty but a lot finer and shorter than coconut and difficult to weave. Ginger and I wove fanciful birds and stars to stick on top.

"Let's go!" Reports drifted in that Haleiwa and Sunset were thirty feet on the far north shore. We drove through pineapple and sugarcane fields to get there. Daddy and Flippy Hoffman consulted on the beach as to the best way to tackle the big surf at Haleiwa. It breaks far out and they would have to paddle over a mile. My dad recalled surfing there in the 1930s in thirty-five-foot swells and losing his board. It was a long way to swim. Recently on the David Letterman show he told this story adding that he had his wife with him tandem. I was shocked as this came over the air waves because I had never heard that before. David said, "That's nice. He took the little woman along." That would have been Muriel, my mother.

He and Flippy decided they should tie fins around their waists in case they had to swim a long distance. As they paddled out of sight it was a little unnerving for us

The Kukeas—Mele, Ethel, Kala and Kahele.

on the beach not to be able to see them. Although I had complete faith in my father, we all spent a restless afternoon until they both paddled safely back into the bay. It was hard to get a perspective on how big the waves really were from the beach.

Daddy was wound up tight as a drum. He said, "They are really hump'n out there and the hot curl board was red hot." But after a few fabulous rides it began to get blown out, the waves started breaking all the way across and it became too dangerous.

Cecelia and Lorrin with the first tow-head babies.

Waimea, Haleiwa and Sunset were beautiful, but I didn't like not being able to watch the surfing. I felt like I missed all the action. We stopped in the pineapple fields on the way home and picked several to eat. Yum! They were sweet. My mouth burned for two days from the strong acid.

Lorrin thought it would be neat to drive around Kaena Point. He had heard it could be done. So we all loaded in the Chuck-a-luck along with a couple of other guys that thought it would be a fun adventure. It was, for a while. as we edged above the ocean on the side of the cliffs, the

Lorrin and "Laho Lio" tandem at Corona del Mar.

rough little dirt road becoming narrower and narrower. Finally we reached a spot where most of it had crumbled away. We all bailed out and inspected the situation. It took almost an act of God to persuade my dad that this jaunt was not going to be possible. He hated giving up on any wild idea he set his mind to.

When we got back to Makaha, no tent. It had blown away. We soon discovered the locals had found it. They brought it down to us and set it up all over again.

Usually when the surf was up on the north shore Waikiki was flat and vice versa. But sometimes it was lousy both places, blown out or too rainy. That's when we took a trip around the whole island. Other than several flat tires we didn't have too much trouble with the big black Chuck-a-luck. We checked out the Pali, body-surfed at Makapuu and watched the blow hole.

The Hawaiian boys at Waikiki seemed to be always clowning and playing. They took dogs, chairs, and towels for sails out on their boards, and wore all manner of hats. One guy had a hat made out of a pant leg. It was a circus every day. They had a serious side too. They were excellent lifeguards. When the surf was up we witnessed more than one rescue. Even on their days off they didn't miss a swimmer in trouble. My dad spotted them quickly as well, but then he had been a lifeguard for many years at Santa Monica.

It was time to launch the new skiff in front of the tavern. We went fishing and diving out past the Queens. The little boat worked splendid and even caught a few waves on the way in. Beachboys pointed and rocked with laughter, "Whitey, papa he'e nalu wid da boat."

Each day was filled with fun surfing, fishing, canoeing, hula lessons. Sometimes we swamped the canoes. We laughed so hard it was difficult not to choke on the salty water. We had to bail like crazy with buckets to get water out of the canoe if a wave broke on it. Daddy even went with the guys to the dock when the Lurline came in to dive for coins. Evenings were filled with good food and song. Many of them were spent at the Edgewater watching Johnny Ernstberg. He and my dad went to the Pali to find just the right Hau tree limbs to ship home for our outrigger iakus arms.

The night before we left, Walt Hoffman showed us films of big surf at Makaha and Sunset and we played and sang until 2:30 a.m.

"Boat Day!" "Quick get packed up. We gotta go to the beach first." Daddy was telling us as we hustled around trying to find a slipper, bathing suits, souvenirs, etc. Ethel stayed home to make leis.

The normally laughing dark eyes were sad that we were leaving Kuhio. Strong arms hugged each one of us as they wished us a safe voyage and told us to return quickly. "You come back Wiki Wiki?" The colorful names and faces swam in my mind like the gentle tides drifting in and out.

Aloha

We boarded the Lurline to discover many of our friends waiting for us at the swimming pool to see us off. They showered us with leis and kisses. Clarence Eben moved us to tears with his rendition of "Aloha Oe." Then we all threw coins to the divers as we pulled out of the dock.

We threw our leis outside of Waikiki. As we watched them drift toward shore on the current we were assured that we would return someday. Blackout and his crew paddled his outrigger out into the steamer lane off Diamond Head to wish us Aloha. We watched it longingly until it faded out of sight and the islands disappeared into the sunset.

We were kama'ainas (old hands) now. We were asked to do the hula and have pictures taken of us dancing. We took ukulele classes and participated in other tourist events. A big cake and party was in order to celebrate Jen's second birthday.

Even though I was looking forward to going home, a part of me would remain forever in paradise.

Surfer's Daughter

C H A P T E R V

Whoa! Brown skin girl in the middle of March. I was so dark I looked almost out of place at school. All the kids looked sickly white to me. We had just been home a few weeks when the storm hit. March going out like a lion. Daddy had the San Juan moored to the Capo Beach Pier. The wind was howling and the sea was rough when we went to check on it that night. It was so dark it was difficult to see, but my dad's fear was not unwarranted. It had broken the moorings and slammed against the pier. Halfway into shore we could barely see the bow still floating in the stormy breaks. The entire stern must have been broken and under water. We ran along the beach yelling in the wind and the night, salvaging what we could, hose, rope, boxes, and buckets, but much was lost.

Life often seems a balance scale to me. Along with the good comes the bad. Seems to be inevitable. This was a devastating blow to our family. After the expense of the vacation our livelihood seemed literally on the rocks.

The next day what was left of the boat was hauled ashore for repairs and rebuilding. Daddy and Dave Tompkins dove for abs that spring and summer from a skiff. It seemed like a great lesson in dealing with adversity to me. Listening to the adults that stormy night, I was sure life was coming to an end as I knew it, but I discovered it does go on. We mend the broken pieces and make do as best we can.

Soon the San Juan II was ready to be christened and launched. Some of the original equipment had been replaced but most of it was just "Mickey Moused" back together.

It seemed that the air compressor never worked well from that time on. But there was never any talk of buying a new one. If Daddy was down diving and it cut out, he just popped to the surface somewhere pulling his face

Art Lavaghino, Eddie McBride, Lorrin Harrison, "Straight Off," Andy Jahan gettin' together at Onofre

mask off, gulping air and often laughing at whoever was on deck in a panic trying to get it started up again. He would climb aboard and putz around with it until he got it going.

That summer was fascinating to me. Our weekend trips to the beach were spent more and more at Doheny rather than San Onofre. There was a new group of guys and some of the old ones that hung out there. The surf

97

Doho family.

was pleasant, a little closer to shore at Doho and a little faster break in front of the lifeguard tower and there were boys, at least two or three close to my age and Ginger's age. This was truly an exciting new revelation to me, boys that surfed. No girls yet except us. There were a few women and wives that attempted it. Doheny was a good learners beach.

The lifeguard, a few teachers on summer vacation and a handful of college boys that worked in the park driving the trash trucks set up a camp made mostly of gunny sacks. This group and friends that came to stay with them talked about surfing concepts. In their camp they pieced together funny little pointed boards out of balsa scraps, fiberglass and resin. These boards were so thrown together they hardly held up for the summer before they got water-logged. What we were watching was a whole new style of surfing just beginning to evolve in its earliest stages.

At first I thought these kids were just doing stunts on their boards. Then I began to realize that they were creating their own style, cutting back and forth on their boards to shoot the curl and walk the nose. We saw the first hang tens, quazimotos, bizarre stance, and antics of this wave play. It did seem to work for the little waves, little guys, and little boards. The old guys laughed on the beach and said, "Look at those crazy kids." They dubbed them "hot doggers."

There were the locals, Rex McMullen, the ranger's son, and his buddy, Danny Brawner. Phil Edwards, from Oceanside, and L.J. Richards spent part of the summer at the gunny sack camp working away on the boards and setting a precedent in style for the rest of the kids. These high school boys would literally play in the surf, something we take for granted today with the kids and surfing. Mickey Dora ("Meatball") appeared occasionally at Doheny and 'Nofre. He had perfected a definite style that influenced all the kids that watched him.

The next summer Hobie had opened his shop on the Coast Highway at Dana Point. This made surfing even more accessible. Since Doheny was just down the hill it became the experimental beach and every new board was tested there. Families with youngsters camped at Doheny and they quickly became interested in surfing. Our family enjoyed the company of many of these folks and they joined our weekend cookouts and parties.

Marian talks of her memories of Doheny and friends: "When we were little we all had surfboards, but all the other kids had surf mats. They were inflatable rubber rafts. They were great because you could catch waves way outside and ride all the way in right up to the beach, and they were soft and spun around. We three little kids were begging for mats because our friends all had them. Daddy always had lots of gunny sacks, burlap bags, for fishing and of course plenty of old inner tubes on hand. One Saturday morning he inflated three tubes and stuffed them into gunny sacks and off we went to the beach. They worked just great, caught waves, and actually steered better than the rubber mats. We didn't even mind our tummies getting itchy and rashy from the burlap."

Then there was the kayak. He made a frame of bamboo and layered gunny sacks over it. It was very important to him to use materials that were readily available to him with no expense involved. He then fiberglassed the outside. He removed the frame and attached one of his surfboard fins. It resembled a sea monster more than a kayak, all lumpy and brown. Everyone in town knew Daddy was a fisherman, so when we stopped at the store with this thing strapped to the top of our car, people came out to see what strange, huge fish he had caught this week. The kayak didn't work that great, but it did catch waves and the kids had fun practicing steering it even if it was embarrassingly ugly."

Little groups of boys began to show up from Windansea to Malibu all along the coast, however it was not crowded by any means. It was still the '50s and we were not aware that surfing was just on the brink of becoming a phenomenon. I was still learning in the style I had been raised with and still being coached on just about every wave by my Dad. As I grew a little bigger and stronger, it really was becoming fun. I would stay out practically all day catching one little wave after another. I was hooked.

The new style was taking advantage of the wave at its strongest point. No long ride. These kids would catch it just as it peaked and began to break, kick the board on an angle, run to the nose then back, and swing it completely around the other direction back into the curl, stall, turn again if the wave was still powerful enough, or pull out.

Marian, Tracy Sizemore, Buster Krueger, Little Lorrin,
Steve Jahan and Clancy, surf dog.

Sometimes they shot back and forth six or seven times.
Other times they pulled out almost as soon as they started.
They were perfecting pullouts. Squatting on the nose
pulling it through or kicking the board around from the
tail slicing through the wave.

How well I remember cold winter mornings! Five kids
ranging in age from four to seventeen years old shivering
in our bathing suits, our boards under our arms. As we
stood there hesitantly at the surf's edge, trying to focus on
the foggy chill of the San Onofre coastline, wiping sleep
from our eyes, teeth chattering, Lorrin hollered exuberantly,
"It's red hot, let's go!"

Classic tandem, right slide.

It was probably just as well that we were half asleep or we may have been more reluctant to do his bidding. Those five boards slapped on that icy cold water along with undisguised moans and groans. Our father just would not take no for an answer.

I was at the age where I was looking at boys and they were looking at me. However, except for an occasional "Hi," they rarely spoke to me. The babysitters were still there. I might as well have been raised in a convent. These old guys kept a discerning eye on every move I made whether my dad was around or not. It was both frustrating and comforting at the same time. I soon became unapproachable.

Teenagers like to talk, laugh, and share experiences with their peers. Ginger was busy with college and working, and didn't get down to the beach as much anymore. The little kids were busy with their friends. I often felt lonely, but not alone. The old guys were always laughing and teasing. I could easily sit with them and share their conversations. After all, this is what I had always done. Sometimes I was able to convince a few girl friends from Tustin to spend a day or a weekend with me at my dad's. Most of the time it was my best friend, Susan. She has fond memories today of surfing tandem with Lorrin and bouncing behind me on Talent down the river bed as we dreamed of being famous artists together in Hawaii. She has become a famous artist and Daddy went to see her more than once in Arizona. She always felt like he was her dad too.

I had just turned fifteen and was tending lines for my dad while he dove that summer. Tending lines meant that I was to stay on the boat and watch for any danger, or if the compressor kicked out I could jerk on the line that he held to signal him. It was attached to a large net bag woven on a metal ring that he filled with abalones. Legally he was supposed to be dressed in a full diving suit with weighted feet and helmet. It was relegated to hang in the barn and never get used. He preferred to dive in trunks and a wool sweater. He made his face mask. It was heavy brass but still considered a lightweight device compared with the old suit helmet. The long black air hose from the compressor was attached to it and it had a valve to release air. The rubber straps that held it on his head made it easy to pull off if he was in a hurry. He was big into using rubber inner tubes for everything. He cut them up and fashioned them with fish line to secure his mask, or goggles, which he preferred, for skin diving. He used them and the string to tie net corks to his hat for floating. There was no end to his inventions for cut-up inner tubes. He never dove too deep, usually 25 to 60 feet. We did see sharks every so often, but there was

Santa Monica Lifeguards. From left: Pete Peterson, Lorrin Harrison, Adie Bayer, Joe Parsons, Duke Hughes, Dexter Wood, Hoppy Swarts, Barney Wilkes, Marold Eyestone.

never any great fear. If they came close, I just signaled with three tugs on the rope. He came to the surface and we went somewhere else. He was also always inventing new diving equipment. One year he had a dry suit, then the first wet suit, I think. He made a net that fit around him like a huge bra that he could fill with abalone. It seemed to work well. The fish, mostly sheephead, couldn't get at it.

We always had a fishing line coiled up on the boat. I would bait the big hook with a glob of abalone meat that the fish loved and throw it over the side while Daddy was diving. I caught lots of big sheephead. We'd go to work about 6:00 a.m. watching the waves as we went out of the cove and came back in. If we were done early enough we would go surfing for a few hours in the afternoon before we started processing.

Daddy continued to build boards and sell them. He always had a project in the works. One day we went to Hobie's to pick up some resin. Grubby and Phil Edwards were there sanding and shaping. Most of the guys were used to me popping in and out with my dad, but apparently Phil had never noticed me before and wanted to know who that was. He was down at our house within a half hour asking me for a date. That was the most fun summer. We surfed together every day possible, shared each wave and each experience. Since I was just barely allowed to date, everywhere I went with him had to be sanctioned by my parents first, and there was a lot I wasn't allowed to do. I was pretty happy just being able to go surfing every day.

Phil had a metallic blue '40 Ford coupe with white leather tuck and roll upholstery, the kind kids went to Tijuana to get, and a new powder blue surfboard. I wasn't sure which of them I was in love with most, him, the car or the board. I had heard what a wild guy he was. I can only say he was a total gentleman with me. In fact, all the guys that I was friends with at the beach were. Old and young were protective, caring, almost chivalrous.

From the time I was a baby I had tandemed with my dad. He always slid me up on the deck of the board pulled my legs apart and layed his chest on my rump with his chin hitting about my lower back. This allowed you to synchronize the paddling together. In tandem the most important thing is to keep the weight of the two people as close together as possible in order to maintain the best control. I was mortified when I hopped on the board spread eagle and Phil quickly snapped my legs together then paddled on his knees straddling them. I don't think it worked so well, but it seemed more appropriate to him, I guess. I never tandemed with anyone that was as good as my dad. Between us it was all instinct.

The babysitters were still on duty, even the ranger. One night Phil Edwards and I were lying on the sand in the park watching as our fire burnt out. We had a sleeping bag thrown over us. I guess it didn't look good to Ranger Woody, another one of the old buddies. He promptly sent me home.

I think I became the wipeout queen. On a nice warm day I would rather be in the water than out, so I was always purposely diving or falling off my board. Sometimes it was tricky to keep your board with you. We didn't have leashes.

It was big surf at Salt Creek, a fast left. Left was not my best suit. I was riding Phil's board, came off a big wave and smacked right into Hobie on his new board. Two dinged up boards and neither of them was mine.

When we went on a date that meant going to Costa Mesa to the nearest drive-in theatre, which was thirty-five miles away from Capo Beach. Usually it was a double feature and didn't start until dark. The earliest I could get home was 12:30 or 1:00 a.m. This was upsetting to Daddy and Lele, and I'm sure it kept them awake discussing it. After surfing all day I was usually exhausted.

One time after I had arrived home and flopped in bed, my dad came and sat down beside me. I guess he was planning to explain something to me as he fumbled around for words about the birds and bees. I assured him that I already knew all about it and he didn't have a thing to worry about. He seemed much relieved to be able to exit quickly. Actually I knew very little about "It," but it was true that he didn't have much to worry about. At fifteen, sex was not high on my list of priorities. Holding hands, a few hugs, and a goodnight kiss would suffice. I was much more interested in going surfing the next day.

As I mentioned before, more than once I would wake up about 5:00 a.m. and ride Talent up to Dana Point to

Top: Vintage boards and boys.

Keen left slide on the green.

Hobie's. At 6:30 a.m. his hooves sounded like guns going off on the cement sidewalk. I wished there was some way to keep them quiet. By then it was daylight and Phil and I would ride double out on the point to check out the surf below. Some days I would ride Talent down to Doheny and he would race along the beach and splash in the water and roll contentedly on the sand.

Daddy began to talk of pollution. Too much sewage was being pumped or was leaking into the ocean as the population of the county grew at a rapid rate. He was very much aware that the detergents were killing the magnificent kelp beds along the coast. The abalones were getting more and more scarce. I listened and he showed me where the sewage entered the sea. White bubbles of scummy stuff floated on the water. But it seemed to me there were still plenty of abs. We still often had big loads we processed until late in the evenings. The fact that the decline seemed gradual was deceptive, for within a few years the detergents wiped out much of the sea life as we had known it.

Grandma and Papa were tired of driving me down to Capistrano, now that Ginger wasn't going down so much. It seemed like too much trouble just to take me. In the winter I was busy with the usual high school social functions, games on Friday, dances on Saturday. But nice weekends or when the surf was up I wanted to be at the beach at least on Sunday.

Ned Leutzinger, my dad's old high school buddy, was appearing regularly at Doheny with his son, Mark. They lived in Costa Mesa and Grandma would concede to take me there so I could catch a ride with them. They were fun to go surfing with. Sometimes we went to Laguna or Trestle. They had new Hobie boards and they let me use them. Mark was a little quiet and shy, but Ned was always teasing and joking enough for all of us.

Good times, good memories, good fun, San Onofre.

My dad was amazingly tolerant of me riding everyone else's boards. We approached the subject just once. He wasn't too pleased, but I couldn't seem to admit that I was uncomfortable with his boards. I always had an excuse, "We didn't have time to come by and pick one up," or "We went to another beach not close by." Having himself been such a renegade as a teenager, I think he was pretty forgiving. He knew I'd come around.

He was doing some real interesting experimentation with molds. He tried making an all-hollow board in a mold just out of fiberglass. I was standing on the cliff at Dana looking down when he took off on a good size wave with the first one of these. As the wave broke on him the board just sort of slid apart like an Oreo cookie. I was embarrassed, but the guys up there watching with me were fascinated. They knew something great was in the works. Groups of those young guys would get together at Hobie's and spend hours brainstorming on new ways to design and make boards.

But Lorrin was on his own. His first hollow fiberglass ones that were successful had a hole with a cork in the tail to drain water that seeped into them. They were not terribly practical and didn't hold up too long. He discovered foam through his older brother, Verne, who worked for an aviation company. It was a very light substance and they had been experimenting and using it for some time in airplane construction.

Everyone was just getting the hang of working with resins and how to mix them. There were paint cans full of it sitting around that had set up so quick the paint brushes were still stuck in the stuff that had turned hard as a rock. Phil and I tried to light one of these cans one night to get our hand warmed. We poured acetone on it and lit it. It kind of blew up, burning our eyelashes and eyebrows off.

Dog days at Dogpatch.

Outfitted in his diving "woolies."

Check out the lines at Dana.

Marian, reluctant participant in the boys' 12 and under contest. San Onofre, 1958.

But if we thought it was tricky, this new foam was totally unpredictable. Daddy made the fiberglass and resin in the mold then tried to fill it with the foam. It didn't always fill completely leaving air pockets and weak spots in the board. He tried just putting foam into the molds. Sometimes it went off, too much foaming out the sides. Kind of like a huge waffle iron with too much or too little batter in it. These molds were big heavy things made of concrete. They were too heavy to lift by hand and had to be hauled around with a block and tackle. They had iron clamps and big nuts and bolts around the edges. One time he was mixing up foam with an egg beater. It went off and exploded all over the place.

Well, some did work and he made me a salmon pink one in the shape of his favorite hot curl board, the "A bomb." One thing I have to say about Daddy's boards, they caught waves easier than any board I had ever ridden. I just had trouble maneuvering them because of the length and the bouyancy, so I found them frustrating.

Grandma and Papa had bought me a salmon pink and white '55 Chevrolet convertible just to drive to school. Wish I still had that. They made it clear that it was theirs and not mine and I wasn't to drive it to the beach, much less take it on surfing safaris. After two wrecks in two months, one going to the beach, they made it even more clear. So I was still hitching rides with friends or riding the bus down to my dad's. Sort of was a shame because that board matched my car, but it stayed down there and the car stayed in Tustin. That board was light and fast, but it was like an air mattress and hard to control. Those big foamies were nice in the winter, though. They floated high.

There were surfing contests along the coast, although at that time there were still more paddling contests than surfing. Most of them were not taken too seriously yet other than the Makaha in Hawaii. Even it was relatively small. Daddy and I won the tandem contest at San Onofre in 1957 beating Linda and Benny Merrill. We received a little trophy about five inches high and got our pictures in the Santa Ana *Register*. It was all in fun. None of us realized that Linda would go on to win national championships or that in just a few years the 'Nofre prizes would include trips to Hawaii, Peru, surf gear, money, etc.

The fishing industry was always fraught with hazards. Tales of them were most often interesting and amusing. Lorrin was on the Capo pier operating the winch when his jeans, which often were well used and tattered, caught in it and ripped totally off of his body. He was standing there stark naked. Two ladies that had been walking on the pier and had been frozen in their tracks aghast at the incredible scene were now attempting to direct their eyes away.

Another time his jeans caught in the winch on the jeep pickup when he and Dave Tompkins had it jacked up to pull the skiff in. It had the same results but at least he was not exposed to the opposite gender. Once the material gets caught it winds around the winch until it tears away or gets completely ripped off. Young Dave, "Brother," was watching this, and thought it was one of the most hilarious scenes he'd ever witnessed.

Decker and Terwilliger were still watching from the bluffs through their binoculars. They finally decided that they had enough of a case against my dad to nail him. New laws were being put into effect with the decrease in the sea life population. Abalones that were undersized, "shorts," should be taken back down and each of them stuck back on the rocks. The Fish and Game wardens filed a claim that Lorrin Harrison was just tossing them overboard. They knew it was him because they could read the numbers on his boat through their spyglasses.

When he was supposed to go to court Dad chose to argue his own case. He and Dave often took out five or six sandwiches a piece for lunch. He claimed that what Decker and Terwilliger were seeing being thrown overboard was the wax paper off of the sandwiches. He also proved that it was not possible from the distance they were away from the boat to discern the small numbers on it. He won! Must have been about this time when he and Decker got into it—really into it! Lorrin was pointing his favorite abalone iron at Decker and yelling at him. Decker grabbed the end of the iron and they were tugging back and forth, toe to toe, the iron between them.

Several years later Decker stopped by the shop—to visit, supposedly. My Dad figured he was just snooping around and chose to ignore him. We were busy processing abs. Decker said "Don't you know who I am? I'm Decker."

The famous Harrison stance.

Daddy looked up from shucking the abs and said, "You're not Decker, you are too fat!"

Since abalone shells and innards are biodegradable (I don't think we had ever heard that word) and they had to be disposed of in some manner, we had little gullies and ravines filled with them on the other side of the hill behind the house. One evening Daddy had come home with a big load from San Diego. After shucking them he was in a hurry to get rid of the shells and guts. He dumped them over the cliff at the cove. There was a little cave in the cliff halfway below. A couple ran out screaming with ab guts stuck all over them and shells hitting them on the head.

Daddy usually had some enterprising idea to keep us kids busy. He decided that we should sell abalone shells in front of the San Juan Mission. Ginger and I did it several times, standing all day by the mission with a big old fish box full of ab shells for fifty cents each. One time the tourists bought all of them. Marian, Lorrin and Jennie continued to do it when they became old enough. Jennie said, "Mom tried to get us to dress up but we decided we sold more shells when we were dressed in our holiest clothes looking like street urchins. We even put signs on the dogs and took them with us." They did great! Sold out every time.

I mentioned before that sculpin spines were poisonous when they stuck you. Someone was stealing lobsters from my dad's traps, so he devised a plan to put sculpin spines all around the door of one of the traps being robbed. Whoever was doing it would really get stuck. All they had to do was watch for the guy with the swollen hand. Once they put a dead opossum in some guy's trap. They got a charge out of hearing the stories about the critter that appeared in so and so's trap that quickly circulated through the small fishing crowd.

Boat building at Huntington Park.

Both Ginger and I decided to marry at a young age. Ginger had been going to college for a while, but I was just eighteen and out of high school. We both married boys from the Midwest, non-surfers, not even real beach lovers. I always wondered if this was some form of denial. My Earl and Ginger's Jim were outdoorsy guys though and into hunting and fishing.

Cecelia, Ginger and I were all pregnant at the same time. Daddy thought that was the greatest thing, all these fat girls sitting on the beach and around his table waiting for their babies. My brother Kelly was born in February 1959, Ginger's Carey in March and my Lane in April of that year. Since I didn't have a mother, and Grandma I don't think ever remembered even having a baby, Lele and I became very close during these pregnancies. I really admired

Tandem take-off, Corona.

the easy, relaxed way that she handled motherhood and she gave me a lot of confidence and advice.

While those first years of marriage were fun, it's almost impossible for a young kid not to feel a little tied down with all the new responsibilities. After Earl had taken a two-week hunting trip, I decided to go to Hawaii with Dad, Lele and the outrigger canoe team for two weeks.

Kelly was eight months old and Lane six months. It was a thirteen-hour flight on an old prop plane out of Burbank. While I was running around at the airport checking in, Earl gave Lane a whole bottle of straight fruit juice that later did not agree with him. Lele and I were still breast feeding, but we decided that we would modestly try using bottles on the plane. We had a package of the new disposable diapers just on the market. They had about the absorbency of a toilet tissue. Neither the bottles or the diapers worked. Kelly wailed half the way over. There was no way he was going to settle for a bottle. Lele finally gave in and discreetly threw a blanket over her shoulder while he nursed. In just a few hours I had gone through every one of those paper diapers and stuffed them in the john.

We slept downstairs in the open basement at Ethel and Joe's. The aroma of the three-day, three-night Fireman Luau going on next door kept us returning there for more coconut milk pudding, LauLau and KauKau. The babies loved poi. The three kids were great babysitters so Lele and I had plenty of time to surf. We spent a lot of time under the cabana of the Outrigger Club staying out of the sun.

At Makaha I went out when the waves were small, but they were hard to catch. Went out again when they were big, but I just floated over them off to the side and watched the guys catch 'em. That was thrill enough. The third week we were supposed to be home, but it rained so hard our plane didn't leave. The flight home was at night, so we all slept—much easier than the flight over.

A few weeks after returning home Dana was up and I made sure I was there. The waves were looking nice. Just right for tandem so Daddy and I went out. We sat out there a long time before one came along that looked steep enough to catch. We paddled for it but couldn't get in. When we turned around there was a big one coming. We had to really stroke to make it over it. It was just toppling at the crest as we went through. We came down hard on the back side, almost like falling and smacking bottom. Then there was an incredibly huge one too far out to make it over. It would break on us if we tried. There was no alternative but to turn around and go for it. This happens often. You go for one of the first waves in a set and don't catch it only to be caught inside in the giant ones that

Mr and Mrs Surfboard, Queen's 1935.

follow it. In smaller surf you can see a whole set coming and paddle out to meet it and it's easier to pick your wave. In this big stuff you can only see the one coming and you may be a victim or a victor.

This was the biggest surf I had ever been out in, eighteen- to twenty-two-foot waves. Lying in a prone position with a twenty-foot wave coming at me, I had the sensation of what it might be like to be lying on a railroad track in front of a freight train. The wave was awesome. I was barely breathing as we turned around and paddled hard. From the time I was just a little girl, I got in the habit of not looking around at the wave as we paddled for it, because it was too frightening seeing it ready to break. Though I had outgrown that habit, this one I definitely was not going to look back at. Once we were in it, I would just wait for my dad's cue to get up, move forward or back.

We were really stroking as the back of the board raised up on the wave. As it broke at the top, the board was forced forward as though being shot from a cannon. No cue! I allowed myself a glance back. No Dad! The big tandem board and I went straight off to the bottom. The huge wave entirely folding. Daddy had been swept off of the back of the board by the tremendous break. It seemed like endless time being tumbled and tumbled. It was difficult to know what was up and what was down. I relaxed and allowed myself to be thrown and tossed in what seemed like an enormous washing machine. There was no use fighting it. Finally I was released to pop to the surface only to be confronted by the next huge soup, gulp some air and dive for the bottom again. Even on the ocean floor I could not escape the tremendous force of those waves. I was tossed around like a rag doll over and over again, returning to the surface in between to catch some more air.

My Dad's only concern was that I might be swept into the jagged rocks that lie off the point close to the surfers. The current pulled me enough to the south to keep me clear of them. Today I could never survive this, but at nineteen I was in pretty top condition. Even so, I felt like a wet noodle by the time I staggered up on the beach laughing.

Ron Drummond has this incredible tandem wipeout on film. Someday I would like to get a video of it. We do have part of that week on video. Daddy is taking baby Kelly out the same as he did Ginger twenty-three years before, holding him up as the little ripples break over the board. He holds Kelly between his legs as he sits on the board and catches the wave then stands him up. Drummond is also on the video surfing his Indian-style canoe in the big waves.

Who Can Say They Surfed In A Hurricane?

C H A P T E R   V I

It was becoming increasingly difficult to make a living fishing, but Lorrin never seemed to be daunted. He was diving more often out of Mission Bay, San Diego area. The avocado trees that he had so diligently planted were growing well, but the market wasn't as great as had been predicted. He had some orders for boards and always had a few going.

It was about this time that Ethel and Joe's oldest son, Kala, came to visit for the summer. He remembers driving home from San Diego with huge loads of abs on the flatbed pickup. "Uncle Lorrin never looked at the road when he was driving." If he was talking to you he had to look at you or he was pointing out the window looking at someone or something. He rarely looked at the highway. Kala held tight as they lurched down the road (no seatbelts) slowing down then speeding up. He would slow down as he became engrossed in the conversation then realize he needed to speed up when he glanced at the road. It was always an up and down ride. Kala described it much like an adventure ride at Disneyland.

Kala says "All my memories of Lorrin are good memories." Even when he talked him into going out surfing at Waikiki in a hurricane. As Kala hesitated Lorrin said, "Come on. Who can say that they surfed in a hurricane?" So they paddled out to Queens and sat in

124

"Lorrin is the best waterman pound for pound or any other way, in the world today."
From We Cover the Waterfront, *1940.*

Ron Drummond, Eddie McBride, Keith Carlsgaard chewing the fat.

the rough storm surf, wind and spray pelting them so hard in the face that they could barely see. The waves were so blown out they were only able to catch a few.

Daddy had taken one of his big foam boards to Hawaii. Some of the beachboys were pretty impressed with it. He contracted with the Outrigger Club to make a whole bunch for them. Each one came out of the mold exactly the same and they were all a bright red color.

Kala recalls helping with these boards: "When the foam started going off in the heavy molds Lorrin yelled at me to run around and tighten all the iron clamps and screw down all the nuts."

The boards were an alternative to fishing and he was also finding other odd jobs. When Kala was in college in New York, Uncle Lorrin called him on the phone, "Hey, I'm in New York. I'm on my way to Dutch Guiana to dive for oil. Come pick me up."

It was the middle of winter, cold and snowing. Kala couldn't leave school so he asked his friend, Enid, on Long Island, if she could meet his uncle and accommodate him. She called Lorrin and gave him directions to her house and he took a cab. What she greeted at the front door could only be described as an apparition. There he stood dressed in full wet suit gear complete with hood. He was freezing and it was all that he had brought with him. Enid needless to say has never forgotten.

Most people who met Lorrin Harrison, even for only a few minutes, never forgot him.

It was those diving trips that almost destroyed his sight in one eye. He didn't like diving in the murky waters at over one hundred feet. He was working at one hundred eighty feet. At one hundred seventy feet he ran out of air. At this depth he was subject to nitrogen narcosis, a feeling of well being, a high caused by nitrogen being pumped into the body. It was probably this, plus the fact that he was always on a natural high that prompted him to believe that he could hold his breath long enough to finish his work down there. When he shot to the surface through the hole in the boat his skin was on fire. He had the bends. No one on board spoke English so he grabbed a couple of oxygen tanks and jumped back through the hole and went down to decompress. He should have allowed for enough air and taken time to decompress on the way up and gas off. He ruptured the retina in his right eye, but he was lucky to be alive. The nitrogen in his blood stream could have gone directly to his heart and killed him instantly.

He was an interesting teacher in that he learned with each one of us when to encourage and when to back off. He didn't push the younger kids as hard or coach quite as much. He just let them get caught up in his enthusiasm to where they truly wanted to surf. Also it was easier for them because the equipment had become much more suitable to their size. They had more incentive as well, because many of their friends were surfing. Occasionally he just couldn't resist prodding one of us off the the beach into the water.

Jennie was probably twelve when he tried to persuade her to go out in ten-foot waves at Dana. She argued, "I can't do that. They're too big." He was so stoked it was hard not to want to share his excitement. He said, "Come on. We're gonna have so much fun. Let's go. It's fine! I'll paddle out with you." When they got out there Jennie was terrified. He said "This is great! I'll see ya." He took off in a big wave and left her all alone out there. When he came back out he explained, "You can't just sit here and you can't paddle in. These waves are going to just kill you! You have to take off and ride one." In this way we learned to be gutsy and not afraid. With a relaxed attitude we learned to think, "So what can happen to us. Maybe fall off, get

Marian and Dad, 1949.

tumbled a little. We can always get back on and try it again."

The crowds had descended on the surfing scene in hordes. It was a chore just to fight the traffic going to the beach on the weekends, much less get out on the waves with a zillion kids going off in every direction. There was a culture evolving from the sport with its own rules, lingo, and apparel. It was the early '60s. The singing group, The Beachboys, popularized it even more with their renditions of surfer music. My dad got a charge out of it all. The more the merrier. He was happy to see anyone enjoying the sport that he loved so much and he was always willing to help new kids learn.

The poke poles were long bamboo with a line the same length attached to the small end. We laid the poles off the end of the boat as we trolled. Holding the poles in our hands we swung them back and forth by our side so that the feather jig on the end of the line would represent a squid swimming.

Wham! The barracuda hit. Each one of us hauled our pole straight up, one after the other, the big barracudas flying in our faces as we launched them on board. What fun! Daddy was really hopping trying to help get them off the hooks and keep the boat running at the same time.

In and out and around the charter boats we went, the people aboard them gaping at us in envy or frustration as the school of fish continued to follow us and we kept pulling them in. Our freezers were always full of bonita and barracuda.

All of us were fascinated with the grab bag of sea life that was pulled up in the lobster traps. Lane liked the octopus that could slide in and out of the trap with ease changing color according to its environment or mood. The eels were interesting to watch too and a little scary. They had to be removed carefully as they could inflict a serious bite. I don't remember eating eels. Sometimes we cooked them up and sold them to a local French family, but octopus we took home boiled and served whole on a platter. We sliced off pieces of the large curled up tentacles and relished the succulent, rich flavor as we ate it plain or dipped in chili sauce. This was undeniably my husband's favorite delicacy of the sea. He preferred it to lobster.

Preparing for a "feed" at Doheny. Lorrin, Jennie, Cecelia and Rosie.

Grandpa Lorrin deftly removed the lobsters from the traps placing them into the gunny sacks that Lane and Kelly held. These were Pacific Coast Spiney lobsters that resemble a large crayfish. They have long feelers and no pinchers. Occasionally there was something else interesting in the bottom of the trap that had to be taken home as a prize. Today it was a beautiful large shell with its inhabitant still residing in it.

Back on the beach Grandpa reached for the shell and held it as he continued jawing away with a fellow fisherman. Kelly and Lane watched horrified as the big hermit crab

Paddleboard races, Santa Monica, 1940s. Ready, set, go!

reached from its lodging. With a snap it had Grandpa's hand in its sharp pincher and poked almost right through it. He let out a yell that surely could be heard all the way to Catalina before he pulled the creature off him.

One day when I was visiting I found my dad out by the shop rummaging around with odd-shaped rocks. Fishing was bad and he had brought those rocks home with the most incredible story. He swore that they were dinosaur fossils. Some were perfectly round spheres, eight to ten inches in diameter. Others were two and three feet long and resembled leg bones of a large animal. He claimed that he had seen an entire herd of dinosaurs lying on the ocean floor all facing north, as though something had frozen them in their tracks millions of years before. It was an interesting theory. I'm not sure that he ever found an authority to corroborate it. He was informed that the rocks were just that, not fossils, but he was convinced that was what they were and continued to bring them home.

He had many adventures during this period. He joined a crew of friends to sail a Rudy Choy catamaran to Hawaii. He fished aboard Miles "Lani" Nesbitt's seventy-foot tuna boat off the coast of Baja. Lani often entertained us at our luaus with his exciting rendition of the Tahitian knife dance. Usually more than one of my dad's old buddies accompanied him on these grueling, physically stressful ventures where one mistake could endanger a whole crew. Ted Sizemore, an ex-cop, and Windy Brown, an old Navy man, were both excellent watermen and enjoyed the company of Lorrin as they worked aboard these boats.

I was told a story of when they were in a school of tuna so large they were not fishable. Daddy hooked into one and went right overboard with it pole and all. Windy wrote a story about Lorrin holding his own among younger, seemingly stronger men and proving his point that from years of experience he knew a great deal more about fishing than they did. One young crewman and Lorrin almost came to blows over how to stack a bait net. The young guy, thinking that he knew it all, got sick of hearing my dad's stories of "back when."

Daddy tried lobstering in Ireland, teaching our methods and learning theirs.

He spoke of diving around a Spanish galleon half buried in the sea floor. He found a huge gold cross that was too heavy for him to lift. He tried to locate it again, but was never able to find the spot where he had seen it.

Photo by Art Brewer, arranged by Dave "Brother" Tompkins. Family, 1976.

Great surf at Corona del Mar, before breakwater.

Sitting around the big table in the kitchen many friends and family enjoyed listening to these tales and more. He talked about the time he really thought that he might not make it. His board pearled in big waves at San Onofre, came down and hit him in the back of the neck. He blacked out briefly, then came to with no feeling in his limbs. He was paralyzed and helpless. Just when he began to pass out again a fellow surfer rescued him on his surfboard and paddled him in. He was fortunate that the paralysis was just temporary. He must have defied "Lady Luck" at least one thousand times in his life span.

It was difficult for landowners and farmers to keep their land in California in the '60s. The taxes escalated with all the progress and construction. Along with the decline of sea life came new laws every year restricting diving and fishing. My dad and Cecelia struggled along with this for about eight years. When they were approached with an offer to lease the land in front of the house for a trailer court it seemed like a sound idea. So out with the avocados and in with the mobiles. Suddenly they were semi-retired. That afforded Lorrin more time to pursue his passions.

They continued to promote and coach the outrigger team and make the trips to Hawaii. Having bought a little property on the Big Island they decided to build a house. It was a kit home delivered by boat in sections and pieces to be put together like a big jigsaw puzzle. The problem was that all the pieces didn't arrive at once or in the right order. They worked hard at it and had a lot of fun as they camped at the beach in Spencer Park. The little house was about ten miles up the road in Kamuela where it was often cool and rainy. So they trundled back and forth every day piecing together what they could as it was delivered to them.

Ginger and I each had three children, all the same ages. She and her family had moved to Montana. I never thought I would want to move away from California because I couldn't bear the thought of leaving the ocean. However, I began to have second thoughts. It seemed like it was taking two hours just to drive ten miles to the beach in the traffic.

We did move into a big old farm house in Orange next door to another old time surfer, Johnny Waters. We were surrounded by about one hundred acres of orange groves that were still intact. Being aware of the fact that the old place including the orange trees was destined to go in just a few years, we took advantage of the time we had there. We raised game birds, had some horses, goats, chickens, cats, dogs, and guinea pigs. Since there was very little space left for wild animals to live in and Waters' grove was more like a jungle, foxes, coyotes, opossums, and other critters seemed to feel at home there too. A fox kept attacking the kids' guinea pigs at night. Earl got tired of it waking us and went out and shot it. The next morning not being sure what to do with a dead fox, I threw it in the freezer.

Grandpa Lorrin thought that was the greatest thing. When he came to visit, the kids would run get the fox and put him on the mantle. He had frozen in perfect running position, tail straight out behind. Eventually we did decide we would move away from California. My dad wanted to know if he could have the fox. Last I heard some fisherman was dumbfounded to find a fox in his lobster trap.

As a going away gift Daddy brought us a gunny sack full of live lobsters and dumped them on the kitchen floor. They slapped and flapped around while the kids delighted in playing with them, something I remembered doing from the time I was very small. We even gave them names before they met their boiling destiny.

Preparing for the move we had been having a big sale and had invited more friends with kids over to help us. We had sold the kitchen table and chairs. A look of total amazement crossed some ladies' faces as they came in the house to buy things and saw all these kids sitting on the floor dipping big lobster tails in bowls of hot butter and scarfing them down.

The plan was that we were moving to Oregon, but we ended up in Montana close to Ginger. With very little knowledge of antiques we bought an antique store. It just seemed like a fun thing to do. Daddy and Lele came to visit us almost every summer. Well, sometimes in the summer. Usually it was spring or fall before or after outrigger season and pretty close to winter either way. My dad would get panicky if it started to snow. He was sure that he was going to be snowbound in Montana for the entire winter. He usually brought palm fronds to weave hats or we picked tules, cattail reeds, or something for him to weave.

Lorrin and Ronald Patterson glassing canoe behind the barn.

Big swell, outside Indicator Reef. Doheny, 1970.

Lorrin with his first canoe, out back of the barn.

He always brought a guitar or uke. He had to keep busy all the time.

We went to California to work for about three to six months every winter so I was able to fit some surfing time in with my dad and get my beach fix.

Ginger recalls the first time they came to visit her, "I looked out my window to see this little pickup and camper almost completely covered with palm limbs. It looked like the Kontiki raft coming up my driveway." We have a friend here that was making porcupine quill jewelry. Lorrin was impressed with her work. So when he saw a dead porcupine in the road even though it was fifty miles from home and it had been there for some time, he had to stop and pick it up for the quills. Needless to say, the smell was almost overwhelming on the trip home. But once he had made up his mind he just couldn't be convinced otherwise. Old habits die hard.

After selling his little house in Costa Mesa and leasing out the land for the trailer park, he and Cecelia were not what I would consider "well to do," but they certainly could now afford the little amenities in life. Daddy still preferred to make do with whatever he had on hand. Bondo, the stuff they use in auto body repair was his latest cure-all for anything that needed repair. He Bondoed his broken glasses, the straps for them, his thong sandals (he always called them "slippers") and of course his hat and the tie for it. He tried it on most anything.

Montana has its share of old-time characters. It's not unusual to see old-time cowboys, overalled farmers and mountain men types in any crowd. But when my daughters and nieces looked up from their basketball game to see their Grandpa sitting in the bleachers in his coconut hat and slippers, they decided he definitely looked out of place.

When we all got together as a family around a table it was noisy. It's one of those families where everyone tries to talk at once and just keeps getting louder and louder and more and more excited. Daddy would talk so loud and so fast when he got engrossed in a good story that he was fairly spitting at you, a habit that I think I'm acquiring with age. I have a friend that was visiting at the same time as him and she can really talk fast. As they were thoroughly enjoying fresh corn out of Ginger's garden, it was funny to watch the two of them face to face telling their stories and spitting corn at each other in their enthusiasm.

I was told one time Lorrin was stuck in heavy traffic so he decided to drive around it in the emergency lane. When he was approached by a cop he talked so fast and hard that he was spitting in the guys face. The policeman just gave him a warning and told him to get back into traffic as he backed away from the open window.

He was making some beautiful boards with the help of "The Fly." Fly was a superb glass man. Building his own boards in the barn, Fly took time to help Daddy finish off some of his since his eyes were getting so bad he couldn't see to do a good finish coat. When I was surfing with him he would tell me to warn him when a big set was coming because he couldn't see it. I swear the man had a sixth sense to compensate for his lack of eyesight, at least where surfing was concerned. He was always paddling out before I would ever tell him to. I certainly didn't notice that he ever had any difficulty catching waves. He caught just as many as ever. I think he could have been completely blind and still surf, he had such a natural feel for it.

Jennie was married to Fly and they lived in a little house on the other side of the railroad tracks. Lorrin and Cecelia had beehives down there and were always making honey in the kitchen. For a lot of years it seemed like the kitchen always included Jen's four little kids getting into gallon jars of honey and peanut butter with lots of the healthful sticky gooey stuff spread anywhere but where it should have been.

Somewhere around this time my dad lost weight. I think he had a bad flu during the winter one year. Then he exhausted so much energy he must have just burned right through muscle tissue. It seemed to me that all at once he was smaller and thinner, but hardly frail even though he might look it. He was wiry, tough, and determined as ever.

One time I picked him up at the San Diego airport on a return trip home from Hawaii with the canoe team. Immediately after exiting the plane, he was running around the airport looking for Hau tree limbs he had put in baggage for outrigger iakus. Lele tried to calm him, assuring him that they would find them somewhere. "How could anyone

Daddy at Breakwater. Kawaihae, age 79.

lose ten-foot tree limbs?" Somehow the limbs did manage
to get sent to LAX but soon a loud message came over the
PA system, "Would someone please pick up the big bag of
sticks in the baggage department." It was the team's canoe
paddles in a large canvas bag. It always was amazing to me
what they managed to transport with them by air to and
from the islands—lamps, rugs, boxes of pots and pans, and
boards, of course, and babies.

Stoked

C H A P T E R   V I I

"This is my church," I remember him saying of the beach, ocean and sky surrounding him on a brilliant Sunday morning. He never pushed us to attend church or take up any religion, but he didn't work on Sunday. That was the day to play. We were all free to make our own choices. I think that is why we all have big windows in our houses and like to be able to see for miles everything that God has created surrounding us. Somehow my dad had his own deal going with Him. I'm sure He smiled down on Lorrin Harrison for all the people in the world that he made happy. One of Daddy's favorite movies I know was *The Ten Commandments.* As his eyesight failed he moved closer and closer to the TV every year to watch Charlton Heston booming out the covenant of the Lord.

In 1983 he and Cecelia gave us tickets to accompany them to Hawaii. By then they had sold the first house they had built in Kamuela and had built two others closer to the ocean. Marian had moved with her family to the Big Island and was living in one of them.

We made a stopover in Maui first to do some sightseeing. The motel we were staying in had a veranda off the second floor room we shared that was surrounded by coconut palms. I woke at about 6 a.m. to a bunch of scuffling noise and a guy shouting from the room next door. My dad at 70 years was hanging in a palm tree cutting fronds for making hats. He climbed back through

Lorrin's favorite two-man canoe. San Onofre, 1985.

the window with them. He was in ecstasy that he had found the perfect limbs.

We went to visit a friend there that resided in a retirement condo on the ocean front. There was just small surf and it was treacherously shallow but Daddy had to borrow a board and go out. Lele was pretty used to this sort of thing. Her only comment was usually, "Oh Gosh," as she shook her head.

No one apparently ever surfed in front of this community because the seniors there all stood up from their lounge chairs and cheered with each wave he took. He responded to the attention by doing 360s, coffins, and more stunts. Always the ham, he just thoroughly enjoyed entertaining people.

Having left Montana in the middle of winter, Earl, not being a water person, was looking forward to the

Collector card of Killer Dana.

crystal clear warm waters and quiet sunny beaches of
Hawaii that he had heard about. No such luck! Surf was
up! On the Big Island this is a rarity and everyone stops
what they are doing to go surfing.

Kelly was visiting also. Being an avid surfer he and my
dad were up at dawn every morning arguing about which
beach to go surfing at. Kelly is an awesome sportsman.
Performing all kinds of feats, he hang glides professionally,
is proficient at sky diving and karate, and he is a great
canoeman. He has little interest in competition other than
the outrigger races. As steersman and coach for several
years, he was one of the best. Watching him surf at Keo
Kea, I thought he could win any contest he'd enter. His
athletic abilities, precision and timing are incredible. He

definitely inherited and expanded on these skills.

He and Dad went to "69" one afternoon that trip and came home with Kelly's board broken in half. Dad's coconut hat was broken through the crown and was hanging around his neck. With tales of huge waves along the rugged lava coastline they settled down and unwound for the evening.

Everyone calls the beach 69. Probably because of a mile marker. It is an obscure private cove with some lovely Hawaiian name like Wailea Bay. Being from a different generation Dad couldn't figure out why all the young guys laughed about 69. Bruce whispered something in his ear. After a moment of realization a big smile slowly emerged and he said, "Oh, too much fun!"

One day we went to "The Mill," where we were to pick up Daddy. We looked over the cliff to see him coming in right on the rocks. He couldn't see well enough to find the little channel. We felt helpless as we watched him push his board toward shore. Trying to navigate the shallow water he cut his shins and feet on the rocks and coral. More than once we laughed as he came out of the water and approached a complete stranger on the beach. Dripping and wiping salt from his eyes he did the "Mr. Magoo" thing, talking away to the baffled person thinking it was one of us. When he finally got close enough to realize it wasn't, he was startled into mumbling something like, "Oh! Oh sorry!"

The following year we had made our annual trek to California when Grandma suffered a stroke. Since she had no one else around, I became the primary care giver. It pretty well tied me down for five months. When she recovered enough that I could leave her for a while, I headed for the beach. It was spring and there was just steady lines of waves at 'Nofre, but it was a little windy and rough. Daddy went out, but he never really made it out there.

Bamboo board rack at San Onofre.

I was puzzled by his unusual behavior. He came back in and dug into the sand for warmth. He said, "I have never felt so tired. It's rough out there. I feel so weak I couldn't get through." We talked about the possibility of him having a cold or the flu. I thought maybe we should get him home.

That weekend our daughter, Shelly, was paddling in the outrigger races at Mission Bay and she invited me to go along. It was a beautiful warm spring day. I thought I'd better take advantage of every chance I could get to go to the beach as we would be leaving to go back to Montana soon. Besides, I would be able to check on my Dad and spend some time with him.

As usual he was popping around laughing between giving directions to the teams and helping carry the boats to and from the bay. While one of the races was going on he lay down on his back and exclaimed, "My chest hurts.

It feels like someone is sitting on it!" I was concerned and asked if he had been sick or had pneumonia. He said, "No, I have just felt real tired." It was impossible to keep him still, though I tried. I kept telling him, "the boys can bring the canoes up, you rest."

The course of the races went from the bay around the breakwater out into the ocean around a buoy and back. Kelly was steering in the men's race and Daddy and Lele decided to walk over to the ocean side to watch them. After he climbed over a sea wall Daddy said, "I'm boiling hot, I'm jumping in the water." Lele took one look at him and ordered, "Sit down right here. I'm going to get the car and don't go in the water."

She first took him to one of those emergency care facilities on the beach. As they waited in line while people were getting bandaids and antiseptic for minor abrasions, the pain in his left arm was becoming more intense. As they proceeded to the front of the line they were told, "we can't do anything for you here. You must go to the hospital a few miles away." They really just made it in time. By the time they got there he was having a massive coronary.

Shelly and I had spent the trip down decorating one of his coconut hats with some beautiful flowers she had left over from an arrangement. We put it on the table beside him with tears in our eyes. He said, "Don't be sad. If I don't make it I've had a great life, the best!" The two weeks before they could accomplish his bypass surgery were really difficult for him. He was supposed to lie still all day. He made a pretense of it. When I came to check on him he was lying in bed listening to the radio. They were playing popular songs from the '30s and '40s and you were supposed to guess the artist and phone in. Since the bedroom is at one end of the house and the phone is clear out in the living room, he was jumping out of bed every ten minutes and running in to phone in his answer. His only concern being that he couldn't get there fast enough.

It seems as though when people face trauma in their lives, it alters their way of viewing the world. Often times older people just give up after a major illness. Others decide to live everyday as though it might be their last. Lorrin chose the latter. He allowed time to rest every day, but he kept busier and happier than ever.

Christmas 1985 we had a family reunion on the Big Island. Almost all of us were there. Ginger and her family, all of my kids and grandkids, Marian and Jennie both lived there with their families so it was a big crowd. Earl and I went over a week early to get in some quiet vacation time before the crowd descended. I ended up staying another week after Christmas with my youngest daughter, Gail, her two children and other grandson just so we could spend more time with Grandpa and Lele.

Daddy had purposely had his little two-man canoe shipped over for the occasion. Of course the surf came up. It seemed to have a magic way of doing that when he arrived on the scene. What fun! He was the only one that was able to handle it in the surf. The rest of us wrecked and did a lot of swamping, laughing and swallowing salt water. It was easy to flip over and try again. Every day for three weeks we partied somewhere, playing ukes and singing Christmas carols until our throats were sore.

Jennie and her friend Bruce were caretakers of a big old plantation house in Hawi. No one was using it for Christmas so we had a wonderful celebration there. Marian's husband, Dave, was skipper on a catamaran for an exclusive resort. He was able to provide a private excursion for just us on a day when it wasn't chartered. We topped an enormous Norfolk pine for a Christmas tree and decorated it with all kinds of seed pods, flowers, and natural things. It was

Patch job.

Old men at Old Man's.

Lorrin stylin' at age 18.

Lorrin still smooth at age 77.

a most joyous and memorable Noel. We all had so much to be thankful for. Mele Kalikimaka.

Spring of 1986, *Eye on LA* was interviewing a group of senior citizens that were all still very physically active in their chosen sports. There was a weight lifter, cowboy, and of course Lorrin "Whitey" Harrison, senior surfer. I still think it is one of the best videos of him. Dallas Raines narrates as they visit the barn, then off to 'Nofre for little waves that my dad is totally stoked about. He points out to sea fairly wiggling with anticipation and says the proverbial, "Let's go! Let's go!" They question him about his heart surgery the year before. He replies, "I feel 100%, like a million dollars." He even got Dallas out for a few rides in the two-man outrigger canoe. That was the beginning of a series of television spots, magazine features, and commercials that kept Daddy flying. We had to laugh when we picked him and Lele up at the airport every year and they were outfitted in new Nike tennies, T-shirts, sweat pants, jackets and caps. When he answered the phone in Hawaii, he said, "Sure, right, Yeah, I'll do it," for ten minutes before he asked, "Who's David Letterman?"

His eyesight was becoming so poor that he almost had to be on top of his hats to weave them. Not only the one eye was damaged, a cataract had formed on the other eye. Eventually he had surgery to remove it and a lens implant to correct it.

Ron Sizemore had a lot of fun playing ukulele with him. He explains it this way. "I enjoyed watching your dad trying to read music before he had his eye surgery and then to see him see without any problem. He used to have to put his face right up to the page to read it before. I think as soon as he was able to see better he started surfing smaller waves. As a small kid I wondered why when sitting in the outrigger he would ask, "Should we go for this one?"

Every summer an outrigger canoe race, "The Whitey Harrison Classic," is held in Daddy's honor. The Dana Point team works hard to promote this event and raise money to support the sport. They have a big feed and party at Doheny State Park after the race and sell T-shirts emblazoned with Whitey Harrison on the back. I was fortunate to be able to attend this event one year.

My dad and I shifted from one foot to the other on the hot blacktop in the harbor as we waited for Lele to return in the escort boat. As it turned out, she came in a different spot so we missed her entirely, but we did get to spend a few hours of quality time together. He was real concerned about getting back to the beach because someone was to meet him there to buy one of his coconut hats. After I made a flying run over to the park to retrieve slippers for our hot feet and discovered the team and Cecelia were waiting for him. I ran back to retrieve him. We had to walk to his pickup first and get the trash bag full of "Whitey" hats. Here is this whole entourage waiting for him to appear and all he could think about was selling some guy a hat for $10. Two darling girls in bikinis approached him and tried to pull him toward a video camera on a tripod. They were pleading with him as he marched by determinedly with the big green plastic bag full of hats.

"I have to hurry, this guy is waiting for me!" he exclaimed.

I stopped him dead in his tracks and tried to get through to his head that these people were trying to film him for the evening news. I had to take away the bag explaining, "I will deliver the hats. You stay here with the girls."

The guy never did show up, but Daddy sold them to everyone else he could on the beach. That made "his" day.

Whitey's favorite pastime, age 80.

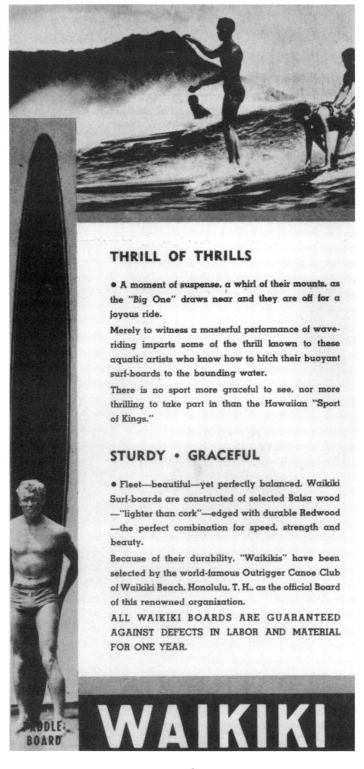

THRILL OF THRILLS

• A moment of suspense, a whirl of their mounts, as the "Big One" draws near and they are off for a joyous ride.

Merely to witness a masterful performance of wave-riding imparts some of the thrill known to these aquatic artists who know how to hitch their buoyant surf-boards to the bounding water.

There is no sport more graceful to see, nor more thrilling to take part in than the Hawaiian "Sport of Kings."

STURDY • GRACEFUL

• Fleet—beautiful—yet perfectly balanced, Waikiki Surf-boards are constructed of selected Balsa wood —"lighter than cork"—edged with durable Redwood —the perfect combination for speed, strength and beauty.

Because of their durability, "Waikikis" have been selected by the world-famous Outrigger Canoe Club of Waikiki Beach, Honolulu, T. H., as the official Board of this renowned organization.

ALL WAIKIKI BOARDS ARE GUARANTEED AGAINST DEFECTS IN LABOR AND MATERIAL FOR ONE YEAR.

PADDLE-BOARD

WAIKIKI

He only came to Montana in the winter once. He and Cecelia brought Marian and her family up for Christmas. The weather was unusually nice. Sunshine, in the 30s, and no wind. Ginger's family is into snowmobiling. They own a snowmobile store in a little town nestled in a mountainous area. We all went there to enjoy the winter sport. It was almost impossible to convince Lorrin that he must wear the appropriate clothing. He insisted that he would not be cold, "I'm used to diving in cold water." We literally had to hold him down and put the insulated coveralls and boots on him. After which we all went out for a long enjoyable ride followed by hot cocoa and tea by the fireplace. He actually had a great time and never complained once about the snow.

We had snow in the fall for our daughter, Shelly's, wedding. He never complained about that either. He was too busy singing and helping entertain the one hundred people that had traveled from all over the world to this obscure little hunting lodge next to the Bob Marshall Wilderness. It was supposed to have been an outdoor wedding, the weather cooperating right up until the day before. But it was a beautiful snow that forced us inside among the poker and pinball machines in the lodge. Nancy Genger, another old-time music lover who played by ear, pounded away on the ancient piano while Lorrin accompanied joyfully on guitar. I think they could have continued the entire weekend if we hadn't stopped them to allow the young people time to enjoy their own music.

There wasn't a trace of arrogance to be found in the man. For all his pleasure at being the center of attention sometimes he seemed almost shy, possessing a sort of sweet humble humility, but he was never reticent. He didn't mind things that weren't perfect. He was aware of the fact that he was less than perfect, but he overcame that with so much gusto it became comical. He had the most marvelous sense of self-esteem without any evidence of pretense. This Peter Pan like quality to his personality seemed to develop even more with age as people thronged around him to listen to him twang on his guitar and croak out his favorite old tunes.

McCrosslin's Boarding House

I'm going to try to tell you so listen unto me
about a famous boarding house on Market Street you see
kept by a man named McCrosslin an Irish man of course
a regular North American European boarding house.
On Sundays we have liver on week days we have mush
and when the bell to dinner rings you ought to see them rush.
There's Jerry Row a man from Galloway, Patty McLoud
and a fellow called Mouse,
tinkers, tailors, cobblers, whalers
all in McCrosslin's boarding house.
When at night you go to bed and try to get some sleep
in walks big O'Conner with his number fifteen feet.
Oh the bed bugs chew they stick like glue
promenade in bands
bottle tail flies get in your eyes and skeeters on your hands.
You ought to see the landlord stare as each one takes a grab,
they demolish everything you have
it would make your poor heart sad
There's Cadakus Flattery just from the Battery
Timothy Rag and Mike McGlue,
Luther Henderson, Capt. Laurery
all in one room number two.
Jerry Row a man from Galloway, Patty McLoud and a
fellow called Mouse tinkers, tailors, cobblers, whalers
all in McCrosslins boarding house.

158

Lorrin and Grubby, kickin' back.

The last time he came to visit Montana, I had to go see an
old lady at the retirement home about antiques. We all
went because we were going to visit 97-year-old grandma
in the hospital next door. I told my dad and Lorrin Jr. that
they had better take their ukes. They might want to play
for the old people. When I finished with the antiques, there
they were strumming and singing away to the oddest looking
group of people in wheel chairs. All of them were wearing
funny hats, some with their heads bent over in sleep, other
listening wistfully and still others singing along. It was hat
day at the extended care facility. Daddy fit right in. He
didn't mind playing for any age audience. Age was never
a barrier to him. Whether they were three years old or one
hundred and three made absolutely no difference.

That evening Ginger had to dance in Great Falls and

they accompanied her, ukuleles in hand. She had not been aware that the performance was to be televised. Also there was a group of senior citizens that were ukulele players. They were thrilled to have Lorrin share his special talents with them. Between dance routines he and Lorrin Jr. played and sang for the camera and we have a nice hour-long tape of the evening. The ukulele group was so taken with his style they have been trying to mimic him ever since.

He and Cecelia were in Hawaii and had just been to the beach for their morning swim when his heart failed. It had been a happy week for him visiting with old friends and beachboys over for the longboard contests. It was as though he just turned out the light. I was with Ginger when Jennie called with the sad news. We were on a plane as soon as possible. All of us six kids, friends and even some of the grands and great grands gathered on the Kona coast to share a week of love and laughter. As each one of us told and retold the old stories and some I hadn't heard before, I couldn't help feeling he would be tapping me on the shoulder any minute, vying for my attention saying, "Rosie, Rosie, guess what I just did."

The memorial service was held in a quiet little cove surrounded by lava and trees. It is used by the outrigger club and is next to the break wall where he liked to surf. In traditional Hawaiian style the women made leis the night before while the men went to rig the canoes. It was a beautiful still morning filled with sunshine and sorrow. Several dozen surfers laden with leis paddled out over the clear water, followed by the four outrigger canoes carrying family and friends. The brilliant colored coral below seemed to reach up to meet his ashes as they were placed into his beloved sea. The thousands of flowers and leis were tossed and strewn together with our moment of

In memory of Joseph Kala Kukea.

Jennie, talkin' story.

Aloha

prayerful thoughts. Then we all leaped into the water to share our tears and hugs in a celebration of his life. Thousands more flowers floated down from a helicopter overhead.

We lingered on the beach savoring the beautiful Hawaiian music under the trees, good food, good friends, and the melancholy of the moment. We watched in awe as the flower leis, palm fronds, and a few coconut hats drifted gently in on the tide wreathing the water's edge on the wet sand creating a huge smile. We couldn't help but feel the presence of Lorrin "Whitey" Harrison.